SO-BCR-942

Commercial Contracts for Managers Series

THE MANAGERS GUIDE TO
UNDERSTANDING COMMONLY USED CONTRACT TERMS: BOILERPLATE CLAUSES

Also available in the *Commercial Contracts for Managers Series:*

- *Understanding Commercial Contract Negotiation*
- *Understanding Confidentiality Agreements*
- *Understanding Effective Contract Evaluation*
- *Understanding Indemnity Clauses*
- *Understanding Tenders*

Commercial Contracts for Managers Series

THE MANAGERS GUIDE TO

UNDERSTANDING COMMONLY USED CONTRACT TERMS: BOILERPLATE CLAUSES

by

Frank Adoranti

Dip Law (BAB), MBA (UNE), FCIS

Solicitor and Barrister of the Supreme Court of
New South Wales

Chartered Secretary

Notary Public

GLOBAL professional *publishing*

First published in Great Britain. 2006
Reprint 2010

GLOBAL PROFESSIONAL PUBLISHING Limited
Random Acres
Slip Mill Lane
Hawkhurst
Cranbrook
Kent TN18 5AD

GLOBAL PROFESSIONAL PUBLISHING believes that the sources of information
upon which the book is based are reliable, and has made every effort
to ensure the complete accuracy of the text. However, neither GLOBAL
PROFESSIONAL PUBLISHING , the author nor any contributor can accept any
legal responsibility whatsoever for consequences that may arise from errors or
omissions or any opinion or advice given.

For full details of Global Professional Publishing titles in
Management, Finance and Banking see our website at:
www.gppbooks.com

© Frank Adoranti, 2006

ISBN 978-0-85297-758-3

Cover Designer: Insignia Graphics

Senior Editor: Jessica Perini

Printed in India by Replika Press Pvt. Ltd.

PREFACE

■■■

Just because you've been signing contracts for years, it doesn't mean you have understood what you've been signing.

One of management's biggest fears is that of an employee exposing the company to the risk of potentially ruinous litigation. It is a fear with genuine foundation.

The cost of litigation is measured in the billions (indeed one estimate is that in the USA alone, the cost is in excess of $200 billion).

A company exposed to litigation suffers the following consequences:

- uncertainty;
- adverse publicity and loss of reputation; and
- expense and drain of management time.

These consequences are the natural enemies of the manager. They undermine the marketplace's perception of the company and can also have adverse effects on a company's share price. This is especially so given the post–Enron/Arthur Andersen climate of business.

During the last eight years, I have devoted much time and effort to instilling a culture of litigation prevention in corporations, by the education of managers in fundamental concepts of commercial contracts.

A common question raised by managers at the conclusion of my seminars is: *What book can I read as a ready reference?* Unfortunately, I found no particular book catering to these aspects of corporate legal education. The most common problems expressed to me regarding existing books on the market were that they were:

- **too difficult to read:** the bulk of titles on the market dealing with contracts are scholarly academic works intended for the practising lawyer or law student;

- **not practical:** the less imposing and shorter "guides" are predominantly aimed at law students "cramming" or revising for examinations or oriented to consumer law issues (neighbourhood disputes, family law, wills and personal bankruptcy); and

- **not portable:** none are presented as handy reference guides specifically tailored to managers. They are usually off-putting in their size, length and/or prohibitive expense.

When discussing the concept of a managers' guide to commercial contracts, most of the comments I received from managers can be summarised in the following quotation:

> *Whilst it might not offer the depth of information on a particular topic that a textbook does, a handy guide in your briefcase accessible <u>when you need it</u> is far better than the volumes sitting on a shelf back at your home or office.*

This provided me with the final impetus to fill the need in this area. You hold in your hands the fourth in a series of books catering to this requirement.

Commercial contracts and boilerplate clauses are an everyday occurrence for just about every business-person and manager.

To the non-lawyer, what is often referred to as "the fine print" in contracts is often shrouded in mystery. Today's commercial contracts are becoming increasingly unwieldy as they attempt to deal with the complex structures of laws, rules and other requirements. This is especially so as contracts tend to cater for an ever-increasing number of contingencies and possibilities. The fine print becomes ever finer.

The purpose of this book is to provide an explanation of the function and operation of the most commonly used contract terms; also called *boilerplate* clauses.

You will firstly be introduced to the "look" of the most common boilerplate clauses, as well as seeing clear demonstrations of when it is appropriate to use them and the rationale for their use.

We will commence with a brief foundation of the structure of a typical commercial contract and examine its various parts and their function. The reader will then gain an understanding of the reasons behind concepts such as using recitals in a contract and the setting of thresholds for any claims made against a warranty, if breached.

Along the way, you will find a number of practical tips on some of the traps and pitfalls involved in the use of particular boilerplate clauses.

As a safeguard, you should *always* seek qualified legal advice in specific situations.

When dealing with the law, often, there is no single "right" answer. This series of books will help managers develop the ability to deal with particular aspects of the ambiguities of contracts. They should be of assistance to every manager dealing with commercial contracts and agreements and from sales and business development staff through to the CEO·

and CFO. The series caters to those in large publicly-listed organisations as well as to smaller businesses.

In writing this series, I have drawn on my 18 years of experience in the law in various countries. I have tried to cut through the mire of theory and "legalese" and distil the essence of a highly technical topic into something easily understandable and digestible for the manager in a hurry.

Where possible, I have used actual examples — taken from situations I have encountered either directly or indirectly — as illustrations of many of the points made in the book. The names, identities and particular circumstances have, of course, been changed in order to protect the confidentiality of those persons and entities.

I trust you find this series of guides as useful to read as I found them enjoyable to write.

FRANK ADORANTI

Sydney, March 2006

ACKNOWLEDGMENTS

■ ■ ■

Naturally, a work which is the product of many years of research and development never comes together single-handedly.

I wish to offer my sincere thanks to Sarah Sieveking for her reviews of the manuscript in its various stages of development. Sarah's many useful comments have been of enormous assistance and have contributed greatly to improving the work.

To my editor, Jessica Perini, who is still with me for the fourth book — continuing to challenge me to constantly improve and refine the message, just when I thought it was not possible to do so. The books' readability and flow have greatly benefited from her guiding hand — particularly so with this volume of the series. I greatly value her contribution to this entire series. If you find this series of books to be highly readable, much of the reason is due to Jessica's considerable efforts, in this regard.

To my brother Gino for his friendship and support.

To my parents; they will always be my treasures and inspiration.

To Kiara, Gianni, Luca and Serena — without a shadow of doubt, the cutest children in the world today and constant source of delight and joy to us. Whatever will they think when they are finally old enough to understand ...

Finally, to my wife and best friend Rosalie, for her love, dedication and unwavering belief in me. My life is so much more worthwhile with her as its centre and focus.

ABOUT THE AUTHOR

■ ■ ■

The author has worked in the private practice of law since 1986. Since 1996 he has worked with a number of multinational corporations both in Europe and in the Asia–Pacific region.

As an international corporate lawyer and consultant, he has reviewed thousands of significant commercial agreements and has seen, first hand, the damage that organisations suffer when proper care is not exercised in negotiating and correctly documenting contract terms. He has also conducted and managed hundreds of millions of dollars of litigation in various parts of the world, caused by such lack of care.

He has been involved in a broad range of commercial transactions ranging from the acquisition and sale of international companies to simple confidentiality agreements, and much else in between. He has also assisted organisations with:

- mergers and acquisitions;

- post-merger integrations;

- corporate restructures;

- establishment of tender and bidding processes;

- crisis management planning;

- contract management systems;

- legal audit and legal risk assessments;

- relations with external lawyers;

- planning corporate legal departments;

- compliance programs; and

- in-house training programs and seminars on contracts and other legal issues.

In addition to his qualifications as a lawyer, he has an MBA and is a Fellow of the Institute of Chartered Secretaries and Administrators. He is also a Notary Public.

TABLE OF CONTENTS

■ ■ ■

Chapter 3   **Time and form of the contract**

Chapter 4   **Ownership of information or property**

INTRODUCTION

■■■

The purpose of this book is two-fold. It aims to familiarise the reader with the look, feel and layout of a contract generally. This is followed by an in-depth examination of particular clauses that are of key importance in commercial contracts.

For many managers and businesspeople, commercial contracts of every type are an everyday part of life. Besides acquisitions or joint ventures and other "major" deals, there are other, seemingly "little" contracts that have to be dealt with. These can range from a hire purchase or lease agreement for a photocopying machine, a fax machine, or a motor vehicle to a contract for the maintenance of a vital piece of plant or machinery.

These contracts, whilst less glamorous than the "big ticket" merger and acquisition deals, are just as important to the continued functioning of the business. They deserve just as much attention and understanding.

Their importance tends to only be appreciated in a moment of crisis. Failure to detect attempts to unfairly transfer risk or miscalculations in contract evaluations can have a lasting impact — often for many years during the life of a contract.

Directors and managers must ensure that adequate processes and systems are in place to ensure that a balance is achieved between winning new business and capitalising on new opportunities and not inadvertently committing an organisation to unduly onerous provisions or accepting an inordinately high level of risk.

Golden Rule

In properly drafting commercial contracts, *preventative* measures and safeguards are the best tools available.

Once you have committed to an unduly onerous contract that is not properly drafted or evaluated, it can often be too late to renegotiate.

You cannot "unring" the proverbial bell.

Neither directors nor managers wish to be exposed to personal liability for having committed their company to a major loss-making contract or one that lacked basic and necessary safeguards.

Worse still would be the case where valuable proprietary rights were actually surrendered or even *given* away.

Depending upon the gravity of such an unfortunate act or omission, litigation could potentially follow from several quarters, almost certainly from shareholders or investors.

Good corporate governance requires that corporations implement proactive programmes and strategies with emphasis on proper contract evaluation and scrutiny in the first place, rather than going into "damage control" after the event.

These factors combine to make a fundamental understanding of commercial contracts and the clauses they contain more relevant than ever.

We will commence by going back to the very basics and examining the key parts of the commercial contract. We will then focus on a number of different and significant contract clauses and issues that typically recur in contract documentation. For example, some of the things we will look at are waiver clauses, assignment and change of control clauses, *force majeure* and dispute resolution issues.

You will see the difference between deal terms and boilerplate clauses.

When you come to the boilerplate clauses section of the contract, there is an important piece of advice to heed; you should not attempt to memorise or rote learn such clauses. This will not assist you.

You should however endeavour to:

1) familiarise yourself with their look (so you can learn to spot them); and

2) begin to understand their impacts and effects; and

3) be aware that some clauses will appear in many different variations and can be worded differently.

The important thing for you is to be able to identify them and understand what is sought to be achieved by having them included within the contract.

When you become more familiar with the look, feel and uses of the various clauses, you should seek to develop an understanding of how subtle differences in their wording can considerably alter their meaning.

Boilerplate clauses are often added or produced at the end of contract negotiations. It is often the final copy for execution of a contract that — paradoxically — receives the least attention. By this point, the parties are so often tired and relieved at having "struck a deal", that boilerplate clauses receive scant attention. The document has gone through a succession of drafts that have been read and re-read; people grow sick at the sight of it. Also, by this point, people regard themselves as being so familiar with the document, that they imagine less care is required with the detail.

Most executives will only carefully scrutinise the commercial or deal terms of the contract. They usually choose to leave the rest "for the lawyers to sort out".

However, the boilerplate clauses will usually govern or regulate the other commercial or "deal" clauses. Therefore, boilerplate clauses play a very important part in the contract as a whole.

Having a rudimentary understanding of the way they work and the way they are used, will place you well ahead of most other business executives in this area.

Chapter 1

FOUNDATION

■ ■ ■

A commercial contract is made up of various components. A typical contract will generally consist of the following parts:

- the full legal names of the parties;

- recitals;

- definitions;

- "deal" terms;

- "boilerplate" clauses;

- execution clauses; and

- schedules.

These will be discussed in greater detail later in this chapter.

■ ■ ■

What is "boilerplate"?

Boilerplate is a term commonly used in the legal profession. A boilerplate clause is from that category of contract clauses, considered to be "standard language", which does not often change from one contract document to another.

The term is said to originate from the newspaper business. It relates to the practice (at the time) of news agencies in the United States supplying advertisements and syndicated material to newspapers around the country in a prefabricated form of matrix, into which boiling lead was poured to create the printing plates.

Since such "boilerplate" text could not be altered, the legal profession adopted the word when referring to the parts of the contract that would not be changed from one contract document to another.

DISCLAIMER

Please use the clauses in this book ONLY as a guide to learning to identify and understand the concepts and issues discussed. It is important that such clauses are not mindlessly cut-and-pasted into documents, without a detailed understanding of their full nature and import.

> This is why I continually emphasise the need for qualified legal advice in your particular jurisdiction, taking into account all the circumstances (and often, the more subtle nuances) of your particular situation.

As the book is dedicated to the issue of boilerplate contract clauses, it is appropriate to consider a number of issues and pitfalls that regularly arise in the drafting of such clauses.

■ ■ ■

Parts of a commercial contract

Boilerplate clauses are one component part of a commercial contract.

The entire focus of this volume is to demonstrate the significance of boilerplate clauses and to highlight the important governing, structural and regulatory role that boilerplate clauses play in a commercial contract.

The other component parts of the contract will also be briefly explained, to enable you to better understand the context in which boilerplate actually "sits". A more detailed discussion of the individual component parts of a commercial contract can be found in ***Understanding Commercial Contract Evaluation***, the sixth volume in the *Commercial Contracts for Managers Series*.

Recitals

Recitals set the background and help give some context to the transaction, which is the subject of the contract. It could also be said to be an executive summary of the nature, background and context of a contract (but generally not of the particular terms of the deal).

Whilst *recitals* set the background and help give some context to the transaction, they can also be a convenient way of recording the parties' intentions, which could become valuable interpretation tools for a court in the event of a dispute.

Recitals are not an *operative* part of the contract. However, a court may consider them (if relevant) in deciding upon an interpretation of a particular part of the contract in dispute.

Definitions

The *definitions* section defines certain specific terms in the agreement. It should be contained in the operative part of the agreement and not with the recitals. This is because the definitions section defines terms that actually form part of the agreement.

Capitalised terms in an agreement (aside from proper names) are usually a prompt for the reader to refer to the definitions section for a full definition of the term.

Substantive clauses

There are two categories of substantive clauses:

- **deal terms**; and

- **boilerplate**.

"Deal" terms

Deal terms are what the contract is all about. These are the terms of the commercial deal to which the parties have come together and agreed.

Deal terms will detail:

- what one party will do for the other — that is, supply certain goods and/or perform certain services;

- the term of the agreement. For example, whether the agreement is for a term of one year with an option to renew, for three years with no option to renew, etc;

- the time limits within which such goods must be supplied or such services must be performed;

- the specifications which the supplier must meet and standards to which the goods and/or the services must adhere or conform;

- what is to happen in the event that such time limits, specifications or standards are not met; and

- the agreed price to be paid for the fulfilment of the supply side of the contract as well as any mechanism for the adjustment of the price, if necessary.

These terms are peculiar to each deal and reflect the parties' agreement for that particular transaction. That is, the deal terms will typically reflect the bargain the parties have agreed to and "shaken hands" upon.

"Boilerplate" clauses

The commercial or deal terms of the contract tend to receive the most careful scrutiny within an organisation, with the rest (eg, *boilerplate* clauses) being largely left "for the lawyers to sort out". Because boilerplate clauses tend to be added or produced at the end of contract negotiations, they often receive scant attention.

However, boilerplate clauses play a pivotal part in a contract, as it is the boilerplate clauses that govern or regulate the other commercial or deal terms.

Accordingly, given their significance, this book is dedicated to and focuses on boilerplate clauses.

Warranties

A *warranty* is an assurance or promise in a contract. It usually relates to assurances about past or present facts in the particular transaction, the subject of the contract.

The purpose of the warranty is to give the recipient of that warranty the right to sue for damages, if such assurance later proves untrue or inaccurate.

The breach of a warranty gives rise to a claim for damages.

The ultimate effect of such common law rules is that the recipient of the warranty may recover *substantially less* than all losses connected with the breach.

A properly worded and well-worded indemnity, instead, can make the *entire* loss recoverable.

For a more in-depth treatment of indemnity clauses as well to see detailed examples, you should consult **Understanding Indemnity Clauses**, the first volume in the *Commercial Contracts for Managers Series*.

Execution clauses

The *execution* clause is the section signed by the parties. It is usually preceded by wording "introducing" the signatures as follows:

> *IN WITNESS WHEREOF, the parties hereto have caused their duly authorised representatives to execute this Agreement as at the date first above written.*

The execution section is the place where the contract is signed. There are different methods of execution for both individuals or companies.

The relevant companies legislation in each jurisdiction prescribes the correct manner and form for a company to execute documents.

In Australia, the law entitles one to assume that a document has been properly executed by the company if done in the manner described.

Headings

Headings to clauses and sections serve as a convenience and as an aid to reading. To have them forming part of the contract can over-complicate any question of interpretation of a particular section or sections.

Prudent drafting should always include a clause to the effect that:

> *The headings in this Agreement are for ease of reference only and shall not be considered in the construction or interpretation of any provision hereof.*

OR

> *Headings are for convenience only and do not affect interpretation.*

Schedules

Schedules should always be expressly incorporated as a substantive part of a contract.

Their purpose is to separate much of the deal–specific detail from the boilerplate sections. They are much-used in standard form agreements. Any deal-specific tailoring of the agreement is then done in the schedules.

They usually contain things such as:

- product and/or service specifications;
- key performance indicators;
- warranties;
- disclosure items;
- asset lists or registers;
- lists of employees; and
- any forms the parties will need to use between one another during the course of the transaction.

Disclosure letter

A *disclosure letter* is most commonly used in an agreement for the sale of a business or company. Its purpose is to make disclosures against the warranties contained (often in one of the schedules) to the contract.

Some agreements often contemplate that a vendor will disclose, to the purchaser, certain matters that would (or could) otherwise give rise to a claim under the warranties.

The effect of this disclosure will be that the purchaser will be unable to use any of the disclosed matters as the basis for a claim under the warranties.

The disclosure letter can sometimes be the subject of intense negotiations.

■ ■ ■

"Plain English" drafting or old-fashioned "legalese"?

Contract drafting styles seem to be polarised between either the newer style "plain English" documents or the more traditional "legalese".

The older style drafting tends to use archaic language and expressions, which are not generally familiar to the non-lawyer.

In traditional drafting, the paramount consideration is the legal effect of the words used. Ease of reading is a distinctly secondary consideration. This style involves the use of long unbroken paragraphs without so much as a comma separating the text. Clauses sometimes have to be read more than once to be properly understood.

On the other hand, in plain English drafting (by its very definition), ease of reading also becomes a primary objective. With both considerations in mind, drafting can become an arduous task.

In some jurisdictions, it seems that "legalese" tends to dominate drafting styles, since many lawyers tend to be comfortable and familiar with what they often justify as "tried and tested" phrases in documents.

■ ■ ■

Use of indefinite words

There is a h-u-g-e difference between what may be considered *reasonable* or *substantial* by different people. Words such as *reasonable* and *substantial* are often used in contracts to express measures of time and quantity. It must be understood that these terms are entirely subjective and mean different things to different people.

A fair question when confronted with either term is:

Relative to what?

Answers will differ depending upon the person answering them.

One would expect that a *"substantial* price increase" in a contract would carry a different meaning for a large multinational corporation than it would for a small privately held company.

The point is that words such as these are not conducive to certainty. A common theme you will find recurring in the *Commercial Contracts for Managers Series* is the following:

Uncertainty is the enemy of the business-person.

Uncertainty encourages the search for loopholes. It promotes litigation. You should strive to avoid vague, uncertain and ambiguous words in contracts. Be on the lookout for them and when you find them, push for the appropriate changes to be made to them.

A properly drawn contract defines and clarifies issues. So when you next see wording in a clause of a contract which states:

> ***Fred*** *grants **Ginger** <u>a reasonable period of time</u> to remedy any defect brought to her attention.*

You might consider changing this to a more definitive time period such as:

> ***Fred*** *grants **Ginger** <u>seven days</u> to remedy any defect brought to her attention.*

If it is not possible to state a fixed period of time, a further qualification to the word "reasonable" can be of assistance in interpreting the word. For example:

> ***Fred*** *grants **Ginger** a reasonable period of time <u>having regard to the nature of such defect</u> to remedy any defect brought to her attention.*

So if the defect were a minor one, the period of time required would be shorter than if the defect were a major one.

It is useful to keep this principle in mind when the time comes to actually draw up the contract.

Golden Rule

Indefinite words such as *reasonable* and *substantial* (and other similar words) cannot be used as objective measures or reference points.

■■■

Ambiguous words

Drafting contracts is easy.

Drafting contracts that will withstand the test of litigation — or are clear enough to actually avoid it — can be extremely difficult.

It is particularly important if your side in a transaction is the one drafting the contract. This is because courts in most jurisdictions tend to operate on the rule that any ambiguity will be construed **against** the party drafting the contract.

If you are the party which exercised control over the drafting and a provision is capable of more than one interpretation, you are placed in an awkward position when trying to assert *your* interpretation over any other; a judge may be entitled to reject your argument by saying: *If that is what you really meant, you would have actually said it that way in the first place!*

It sounds trite but it bears repeating: *say what you want and say it clearly*.

Verbose drafting

The more words you use to express a simple intention, the more potential ambiguity you create.

This may then make it possible for the other party to ask the court to favour its interpretation over yours.

To illustrate the point, consider a sign reading as follows:

> *As this surface has recently received a fresh application of paint to its entire surface, and given the fact that the coat of paint applied thereon has not yet fully and completely dried in accordance with the manufacturer's recommendations, you are advised in the strongest possible terms to avoid any contact with such surface and to refrain from touching the surface directly or with another object until such painted surface has thoroughly and completely dried.*

Complicated isn't it? Even though it appears exhaustive and thorough, one might still ask, how long ago it was actually painted? How long is the recommended drying time? And so forth. Indeed, by the time you had finished reading it, you may have already sat down, leaned-on or walked onto the wet surface. The more unnecessary words used, the greater the possibility for errors arising.

Consider the effect of the same sign using simplified and more direct language, leaving little room for error or misinterpretation:

WET PAINT — DO NOT TOUCH

> ### *Golden Rule*
>
> The greatest control over implied terms is achieved by carefully drafting express terms to be as clear and unambiguous as possible.
>
> Then, expressly disclaim all else.

Any court looking at your contract should be able to establish all of the terms of the deal from just reading the contract (and not having to look at anything else or hear from anyone else). The court should also be able to gain an understanding of the parties' intentions of what they wished the document to achieve.

If you do not clearly express what you require in a contract document, you run the risk of a court implying terms into the agreement that may well be contrary to your original intentions.

As you have seen in the section above, courts have the power to imply a term into the contract where the circumstances warrant. Courts will generally ask *whether the parties would have agreed to it*. An investigation into the parties' presumed intention is a necessary part of this process. The test is *not* whether it would have been reasonable for them to do so.

You have a greater power at your disposal to avoid the intervention of a court: by using clear and unambiguous drafting of contract terms.

A corollary of that rule applies here; economy of words. Do not be tempted to say in 50 words what can be better said in ten.

A frequent argument used by those prone to verbose contract drafting, is the proposition that the extra words "don't alter the effect" or "don't change the interpretation".

However, there is always a chance that they *might*.

Even assuming that the use of such extra words does not have any adverse effect on meaning, there is no place for redundant wording.

More often than not, such extra and unnecessary wording tends to be contained in a precedent document retrieved "from the shelf". Laziness in redrafting or tailoring such a precedent document often accounts for the use of excess verbiage in boilerplate clauses.

Golden Rule

In most jurisdictions, courts will generally construe any ambiguity **against** the party drafting the contract.

■ ■ ■

Implied terms

Contracts cannot possibly provide for every conceivable eventuality or possible permutation of circumstances. Implied terms can arise when a situation or particular event is not dealt with by an express term or where it may be unclear from the contract itself how this is to be dealt with.

Implied terms do not appear in an agreement as do *express* terms. However, their existence and effect in particular circumstances must be understood when drafting or considering any commercial agreement.

Implied terms can arise in the following circumstances:

- **To give business efficacy to the contract**
  It becomes necessary for a court to imply terms into a contract when the parties fail to incorporate terms to cover a particular situation. When a court does so, it must imply appropriate terms that accord with the presumed intentions of the parties.

  This principle of *business efficacy* was first laid down in an 1889 case in the UK. It is an accepted part of most common law jurisdictions today. Any term *implied* into a contract by the court must be:
  1) reasonable and equitable;
  2) necessary — without which the contract would be ineffective;

3) so obvious that it "goes without saying";

4) capable of clear expression; and

5) must not contradict any express term of the contract.

- **Because of a custom or trade usage**

  This arises where one or both of the parties are engaged in a particular industry or trade. In such a case, the customs or usages of that industry or trade may be implied into the contract.

- **Terms implied by statute**

  Numerous statutes imply terms into contracts. Usually such statutes make it illegal to attempt to contract out of or attempt to exclude any rights created by the statute.

  In Australia, the most common examples are the *Sale of Goods Act* and the *Trade Practices Act*, which imply terms as to quality and fitness for purpose into certain contracts for the sale of goods.

- **Terms implied through a *course of dealing between the parties***

  In attempting to interpret the parties' intentions, a court may have regard to the past dealings of the parties. A court may imply terms into a contract under this category, by considering:

  1) the length of time over which dealings had been conducted; and

  2) the consistency of the previous conduct that the court is being asked to imply into the current agreement.

Chapter 2

PARTIES TO THE CONTRACT

■ ■ ■

There are a number of fundamentals that must be correct in the contract, before you even consider the terms. One of these is the correct identification of all of the parties to the agreement. There is no room for even the slightest error in this regard.

A misconception amongst a small number of managers is that a mere reference to an entity within the body of a document is sufficient to bind that entity to an enforceable obligation — even if that entity is not actually a party to the contract.

In this chapter, we will examine some of the more common forms of legal entities and look at the advantages of using such an entity or structure. We will also look at the problems encountered when an entity is not correctly identified in a contract.

Along the way, we will look at some boilerplate clauses associated with the selection and use of particular entities. Some of these clauses are simply used to overcome logistical problems in having a document executed (*counterparts clause*), whilst other clauses are more significant in being used to avoid unintended relationships (*no partnership or agency clause*), or to overcome problems of an entity lacking in substance and means (*guarantee clause*).

■ ■ ■

Describing the parties

The first part of any agreement clearly refers to, and defines, the parties to the contract. This part of the contract also sets out and defines how they are to be referred to throughout the agreement.

In the days of manual typewriters, it was customary to abbreviate names of parties to something more manageable. With the advent of word processing this is not a necessity, however, it still makes for much easier reading. For this reason, abbreviations are universally observed. For example, a party to a contract might be named in the following way:

The Widget Manufacturing Company Limited ("WMCL")

OR

> *The Widget Manufacturing Company Limited
> (hereinafter referred to as "WMCL")*

Alternatively, the abbreviated form of reference to a party might, more conveniently, refer to their role in the particular transaction, the subject of the contract. For example:

> *The Widget Manufacturing Company Limited
> ("Purchaser")*

OR

> *The Widget Manufacturing Company Limited
> (hereinafter referred to as the "Purchaser")*

Although it does little to facilitate the reading of a contract document, some traditionalists still prefer to use the archaic form of expression:

> *The Widget Manufacturing Company Limited (of
> the first part)*

OR

> *The Widget Manufacturing Company Limited
> (hereinafter referred to as the party of the first part)*

It is good drafting practice (and makes for much easier reading) to define the parties at the beginning and use a convenient and under-standable abbreviated form for reference throughout the document.

Another term worthy of its own separate definition is the word "party" or "parties". This facilitates the use of the following words within the contract:

- the word "party" — for example:

    *If either **party** breaches the contract*

    could be defined to mean "the Vendor or Purchaser, as the case may be".

- the word "parties" — for example:

    the parties shall resolve the dispute in the following manner

    could be defined to mean "the Vendor and Purchaser".

■ ■ ■

Correctly identifying the parties

Having understood how the parties are defined, we must ensure that we refer to the correct legal entity when contracting with another party.

When entering into a contract with another party, the correct *description* of that other party on the contract document is of *vital* importance. This is a part of the agreement that can sometimes escape scrutiny. Changing a single word (or, sometimes, even a single letter) in the name of an entity, could have you contracting with a completely different entity to the one with which you originally thought you were dealing. This could ultimately make the difference between having recourse to an entity of substance and an empty shell.

If a party to a contract is not correctly identified, you risk the following consequences:

- you may not be able to enforce your rights under the contract against the other party; or

- the legal entity you have actually contracted with is different to the one with which you originally negotiated.

Case study:
With whom am I contracting?

Correctly naming the parties to a contract

Lossmakers Limited ("**Lossmakers**"), an Australian public company, was the head Contractor in a major government works project. **Lossmakers** needed to sub-contract a number of crucial and highly specialised works in that project.

Given the complex nature of those works, **Ian Eppt**, the Chief Executive of **Lossmakers** spent several weeks personally negotiating with **Mick Arno**. **Mick** identified himself as the Principal of a firm known as **Mick Arno Engineering**.

At the conclusion of negotiations, **Ian** had his secretary issue **Mick** with **Lossmakers'** standard printed form of contract conditions. **Ian** had his secretary insert the details of the sub-contractor on the front page of the contract as:

Mick Arno Engineering
(ACN   )

The words "Proprietary Ltd" or "Limited" or "PLC" or "Inc" did not appear and the space on the printed form of contract to insert the ACN (Australian Company Number) number was left blank.

Therefore, the works were performed by a company that was not named on the contract. They were also performed so negligently that it caused **Lossmakers'** customer (the government) $25 million in damage.

Lossmakers was primarily liable, under the terms of its contract with its customer, to pay such amount to the customer to make good the damage. In addition, **Ian** suffered the humiliation of the government publicly terminating the contract and commencing legal proceedings against **Lossmakers**. The entire loss to **Lossmakers**, including its own lost profits and damage to its reputation, exceeded $100 million. **Lossmakers** sought to recover this amount from the sub-contractor.

In order to do this, **Lossmakers** had to correctly identify the sub-contractor as a legal entity. Under the contract **Mick** (in his personal capacity) was the party named, **not** the company that actually performed the works.

Mick is destitute. The company that performed the services under the contract owns a substantial pool of assets. However, that company was neither a party nor a signatory to the contract.

During the negotiations with **Ian**, was **Mick** representing himself or the company?

The only way for **Lossmakers** to find a solution was to embark upon the lengthy, expensive and highly uncertain process of litigation, that continues to this day.

If only more thought had been given to properly naming the correct parties to the contract ...

■■■

Counterparts clause

Having discussed the parties to a transaction, it is appropriate to deal with an important issue incidental to the parties' execution of a contract.

A useful clause to use, in some circumstances, relating to the execution of documents, is the *counterparts* clause.

Normally, all parties should sign all copies of the agreement.

However, this is not always possible when there are tight deadlines and the parties may be separated by distance. For example, an American company may be entering into an agreement with an Australian company to purchase a business situated in Germany. In this case, lawyers in Germany may be preparing the contract and signatures are required in Germany as well as in the USA and Australia by the respective parent companies of both the purchaser and vendor, in anticipation of completion.

In this case, there may not be time available for all copies of the documents to travel the globe for signature. In that case, a counterparts clause is a useful tool to help shorten the process and ultimately achieve the same result. Such a clause may read as follows:

COUNTERPARTS

This Agreement may be executed in any number of counterparts (including by facsimile) and by the parties to it on separate counterparts, each of which is an original but all of which together constitute one and the same instrument.

■ ■ ■

Legal entities (and some misconceptions)

The type of entity with which you are dealing can have a significant impact on your ability to enforce performance.

We will now briefly examine some of the more common legal entities and structures you may encounter. From this, you will begin to see some of the practical differences emerging.

Sole trader

A *sole trader* is any natural person (male or female) acting by themselves and not under a *legal disability*. Persons under a legal disability include persons who are:

- under the age of 18 years (at law, such persons are referred to as *minors* or *infants*);

- undischarged bankrupts; or

- those of unsound mind.

Partnership

A *partnership* is composed of two or more legal persons, all of whom constitute the partnership.

A partnership, of itself, is *not* a legal entity. The individual partners themselves comprising the partnership are legal entities — whether they are companies or individuals.

At common law, all partners are jointly and severally responsible for the acts of the partnership. This can be a problem where a partner or partners act to purportedly represent the partnership. Partners also owe a *fiduciary duty* to the other partners of the partnership.

However, it is good practice to achieve a valid contract with a partnership, that *all* of the partners be named on the contract. In any dealings with partnerships, it is best to have *all* partners sign the contract.

For more about the nature of a partnership, see the **No partnership or agency clause**, p 42.

Limited liability partnership

Some jurisdictions recognise the concept of a *limited liability partnership*. Somewhat akin to a company, the partners' liability is limited to the extent of their capital contribution.

Unlike a normal common-law partnership, the partners do not have unlimited liability.

Some states in Australia recognise this entity. In New South Wales and Victoria, for example, the partnership is comprised of two or more partners:

- One of the partners must be designated the *general partner*. The general partner is charged with running the day-to-day operation of the partnership's activities and has the authority to bind the partnership.

- The limited partner cannot bind the partnership and has no authority to bind the partnership.

Such partnerships are registered with a government authority (in much the same way as a company is registered). The register records the identities of the partners, their "shareholding" in the partnership and their designation as general or limited partner.

Therefore, anyone doing business with a limited liability partnership can verify the partnership's details by searching the register (in the same way as one would do a search against a company).

Often, the use of limited liability partnerships gives added flexibility in relation to tax planning. As such, it is a vehicle that tends to be used by the more sophisticated multinational corporations.

Registered business name

A *registered business name* is sometimes referred to as a *trading name*.

For example, remember the previous case study where **Lossmakers Limited** purported to enter into a contract with (what it thought was) a business called "**Mick Arno Engineering**".

Notice that the name does not have any form of suffix to identify it as a corporation. See **Company** for examples of corporate suffixes in various countries.

A business name or trading name is not a legal entity. You should not enter into a contract with a registered business name. It is the *owner* of the business name that is the entity with the *legal capacity* to enter into a contract.

You should check the *owner* of the registered name to ascertain whether it is a company, sole trader, partnership etc.

Trust

A *trust* is *not* a legal entity.

You must *not* enter into a contract with a trust. Depending upon the terms of the relevant trust deed (which is effectively the *constitution* document of the trust), it is the trustee of the trust that has the legal capacity to enter into a contract on behalf of the trust it represents.

Company

A *company* is probably the most familiar legal entity. The main feature of a company is that the liability of the shareholders is limited to the extent of their shareholding; that is, to the amount of paid-up capital of such shareholders. It is a separate legal entity from its owners (ie, its shareholders).

The name of a company is followed by the words "Proprietary Limited" or the abbreviations "Pty Ltd". Depending upon the jurisdiction, a company can also be "Limited" or "Ltd".

In Australia for example, the suffix "Pty Ltd" identifies a privately held company (whose shares are not publicly traded on a recognised stock exchange). Whereas, the suffix "Ltd" generally identifies a company whose shares are publicly traded on a recognised stock exchange (sometimes called a public company).

These suffixes will differ in each jurisdiction.

Golden Nugget

Company suffixes in other jurisdictions

- Limited (UK, Hong Kong, Australia, India, Thailand, Bermuda, New Zealand and others)
- Inc or Corporation or Corp (USA)
- NV or BV (Netherlands)

- SpA or Srl or SNC (Italy)
- KK (Japan)
- Sdn Bhd (Malaysia)
- Pty Limited (Australia)
- Pte Limited (Singapore)
- PLC (UK)
- AB (Sweden)
- SA (France)
- AG or GmbH (Germany)
- SA or SL or SLU (Spain)

In Australia, every company has an Australian Company Number (ACN). This number *must* be shown on any contract entered into by that company. Whilst the name of a company can be easily changed, its ACN cannot.

Great care must be taken when contracting with a company (regardless of jurisdiction) to ensure that it has some asset backing in the event of any default. The most basic form of company can be constituted with as little as two dollars of share capital.

Companies are usually registered with the corporate affairs department within the jurisdiction in which it is incorporated. The department is usually a government authority. The registration particulars are public information and can be obtained by a search. In Australia, the department is called the Australian Securities and Investments Commission (ASIC).

Great care should be taken to ensure that there are no charges or judgments registered against the company. This can be checked by a company search.

Checklist: how to protect yourself

There are steps you should always take to avoid the situation involving **Lossmakers Limited** (as described in the earlier case study) from occurring:

- ☑ Always obtain a full and complete description of the legal entity with which you are dealing.

- ☑ Ensure that any description provided is verified. For example, it is prudent to obtain a company search of the company with which you are dealing. In some instances, it might also be appropriate to sight the originals of the certificate of incorporation, registration of business name certificates, or any particular licences necessary for the company to possess.

- ☑ Check for any expiration dates of any such documents to ensure their currency.

- ☑ Verify that any person purporting to be a director is actually a director. This information is obtainable by search.

- ☑ Check the company's name you are given against any letterheads and business cards that you might have received during the course of any negotiations and correspondence. If there are any discrepancies or differences, do not be afraid to ask for an explanation of such differences. Persons exercising good faith in a transaction will not be offended by any such request. It also demonstrates to them that you are attuned to every important detail.

- ☑ Check for any entry on the company's register (that you are searching against) that a company might be in receivership, under administration or have a liquidator appointed.

- ☑ Check for any other signals that a company might be in trouble. Note, for example, if a company has difficulty repaying its debts, or any remarks or other conduct suggesting the company might be in crisis.

■■■

No partnership or agency clause

A prudently-observed rule of contract drafting is to:

> *Draft express terms clearly and unambiguously. Then, expressly disclaim all else.*

This clause is a form of disclaimer. It is intended to expressly rule out any notion, suggestion or implication that the parties may be acting or operating in any sort of partnership.

A *no partnership* or *agency* clause may look like this:

> **Company A** *is an independent contracting entity and does not have authority to act for or to bind* **Company B** *in any way, or to represent that* **Company B** *is in any way responsible for the acts of* **Company A**. *This Agreement does not establish a joint venture, agency or partnership between the parties, nor does it create any employer/employee relationship.*

What it is used for and why

The purpose of such a clause is to expressly rule out any possible implication of a situation arising where one party could assert that a contract conferred certain rights upon it to enter into a binding commitment *on behalf of* another.

This clause deals with potentially the most dangerous kinds of rights; those of having the acts, statement or representations made by another party to a third party binding upon your company.

It is particularly important to expressly disclaim the existence of a partnership:

- firstly, because — at common law — a partner binds all other partners of the partnership *jointly and severally* to any obligations incurred in the name of the partnership or acting as a partner; and

- secondly, partners owe a *fiduciary duty* to one another.

  A relationship is said to be a *fiduciary relationship* where someone is in a position of trust in relation to another (or others) and who must, therefore, act for that person's (or those persons') benefit.

  A *fiduciary* must avoid any situation where that fiduciary could have a personal interest conflicting (or which might conflict) with the interests of those whom the *fiduciary* is bound to protect.

  A fiduciary relationship generally exists between a solicitor and his/her client, a director and the company on whose board that director sits and between partners in a partnership.

Most parties, in a typical arm's-length commercial transaction, will want to expressly rule out the possibility of either event occurring.

The reason for wanting to disclaim the existence of any notion of agency is that any acts or representations made by an agent are binding upon the principal.

It goes without saying that any prudent company would want to eliminate any unintended consequences such as these. As between the parties to the contract, this clause is effective in disclaiming such notions. As against third parties, however, this will be far less effective.

For example, if two parties to a contract, by their actions, create a situation where a third party is led to believe that the parties are in partnership, there is the potential for that to have a binding — yet unintended — effect upon those parties to the original contract.

An important caveat to bear in mind is that courts may often base their decisions on the basis of actual *conduct* of the parties rather than the use of boilerplate wording in a contract.

■ ■ ■

Guarantee of performance

It always pays to consider, prior to entering into a transaction, what could happen if the other party were to default in its performance of the contract. Especially, in the case where the performance of the contract is in a mission critical area, it is often too late to consider the question, at the time it actually arises.

In the appropriate circumstances, a guarantee clause is often of assistance in such contingency planning.

A *guarantee of performance* clause should be differentiated from a typical consumer guarantee where, say, a parent guarantees a child's bank loan.

Given the *Commercial Contracts for Managers Series* is oriented towards commercial situations, we will be more concerned with the situation where a parent company is called upon to guarantee its subsidiary's performance of the terms and conditions of a contract it has entered into.

Such a guarantee can be as simple as:

X guarantees the proper and punctual performance by Y of the terms and conditions of this Agreement such guarantee testified to by X's execution hereof.

Or it can be a more intricate and complex one such as the following:

1. PARENT COMPANY GUARANTEE

1.1   *In consideration of the Purchaser entering into this Agreement, the Vendor's Parent Company unconditionally and irrevocably guarantees as a continuing obligation the proper and punctual performance by the Vendor of all its obligations under or pursuant to this Agreement and any other obligation arising from or incidental to the terms of this Agreement.*

1.2   *The liability of the Parent Company under this Agreement shall not be discharged or impaired by:*

   (i)   *any amendment to or variation of this Agreement, or any waiver of or departure from its terms, or any assignment of it or any part of it, or any document entered into under this Agreement;*

   (ii) *any release of, or granting of time or other indulgence to, the Vendor or any third party, or the existence or validity of any other security taken by the Purchaser, as applicable, in relation to this Agreement or any enforcement of or failure to enforce or the release of any such security;*

   (iii) *any winding up, dissolution, reconstruction, arrangement or reorganisation, legal limitation, incapacity or lack of corporate power or authority or other circumstances of, or any change in the constitution or corporate identity or loss of corporate identity by, the Vendor, or any other person (or any act taken the Vendor in relation to any such event); or*

   (iv) *any other act, event, neglect or omission whatsoever (whether or not known to the Vendor, the Purchaser or the Parent Company) which would or might (but for this clause) operate to impair or discharge the Parent Company's liability under this clause or any obligation of the Vendor or to afford the Parent Company or the Vendor, any legal or equitable defence.*

1.3   *As a separate, additional, continuing and primary obligation, the Parent Company, in consideration of the Purchaser entering into this Agreement, undertakes to the Purchaser to indemnify the Purchaser against any and all losses, claims or costs suffered or incurred by the Purchaser as a result of the Vendor's failure for any reason whatsoever to observe and perform properly and punctually all its obligations under this Agreement (including, without limitation, by reason of the obligations of the Vendor being or becoming void, unenforceable or otherwise invalid under any applicable law).*

Notice that the comprehensive version of the clause has three distinct components:

1)   a statement that the parent will *guarantee* the obligations of the subsidiary;

2)   a statement that the *guarantee will be unaffected* by certain specified events; and

3)   an *indemnity* from the parent company to effectively "bolster" the guarantee.

What it is used for and why

In certain situations, there may be a question mark over the future stability of a company with which you intend to contract. Also the company you intend to contract with might only be a *shelf company.*

> ## *Golden Nugget*
>
> # What is a shelf company?
>
> A *shelf company* refers to a company with only a nominal capital structure — in some jurisdictions, this can be as little as two dollars.
>
> The incorporation of companies in most jurisdictions is a laborious and time-consuming clerical process.
>
> As a consequence, there are organisations that incorporate companies and offer them for sale to those wishing to purchase (usually for reasons of convenience and time) a ready-made company structure.
>
> Until they are sold they are said to be sitting "on a shelf"; hence the term *shelf company*, is applied to such ready-made companies.
>
> Shelf companies are often incorporated with the bare minimum in paid-up capital; as mentioned earlier, depending upon the jurisdiction, this can be as little as two dollars.

When you deal with a shelf company or any company with a nominal or minimal capital structure, you should invariably seek the protection of a larger entity of substance, further up the corporate hierarchy.

Indeed, some organisations are so complex that there are nests and trails of companies leading to the ultimate parent or to at least a parent of some substance. You should not be surprised to find that the immediate parent of a shelf company may be yet another shelf company. You may need to do some "detective work" of your own to:

- either track down a company of substance further up the corporate tree, with which you might, more confidently, enter into a contract; or

- closely verify information provided by the other side to you.

Remember that the single most distinct feature of a company is that its liability is limited to the value of the paid-up capital of its members (shareholders). In the case of a shelf company, where that sum can be as little as two dollars — such an amount would hardly ever be sufficient to give anyone any degree of comfort that such a company could pay for any loss or damage you might sustain, in the event of their default under a contract.

Where it is not possible to contract with a company further up the corporate tree or to contract with the ultimate parent, it is appropriate to seek some form of performance guarantee. Such a guarantee might take the form of a:

- **parent company guarantee** — this consists of a written promise by a parent company to guarantee the obligations of its subsidiary in the event of any default. This requires no immediate financial outlay on the part of the guarantor (in the way of a cash deposit), but does create a *contingent liability* in that parent company's balance sheet;

Golden Rule

Sometimes, in the case of large transactions, it is best to seek a guarantee *directly* from the subsidiary's **ultimate parent company**.

This is especially so when that ultimate parent is publicly listed (and its shares are traded) on a recognised stock exchange.

- **bank guarantee** — this consists of a documentary (and irrevocable) promise by the bank to pay an amount of money (up to the limit specified in the guarantee document) to the party named in the document as the *beneficiary* (or recipient) of the guarantee. Usually such payment is made by the bank to the beneficiary *on demand and without reference to the party giving the guarantee*. Bank guarantees normally require the deposit of cash by the party giving the guarantee into the bank issuing the guarantee;

- **performance bond** — this is similar in effect to the bank guarantee in that it requires the deposit of cash by the party giving the guarantee into a bank account usually controlled by an independent stake-holder. The parties give irrevocable instructions to the stakeholder permitting the stakeholder to also pay all or part of the monies to the beneficiary *on demand and without reference to the party giving the guarantee;*

- **personal guarantee** — when dealing with a private company (one whose shares are not listed or traded on a recognised stock exchange) with a nominal capital structure, it might be appropriate in some circumstances to secure personal guarantees of the directors. The effect of this is to join the director/s, in their *personal* capacity, as parties to the contract. Naturally, in this situation, it is necessary to embark on a similar due diligence as one would on a corporate guarantor. The reason being that you need to be comfortable that the person giving the guarantee has sufficient means and substance with which to honour the guarantee given. An additional feature of the personal guarantee is the fact that a dishonoured personal guarantee could lead to the bankruptcy of the director giving it; in most jurisdictions, bankruptcy disqualifies one from holding the office of director in any company. If the person holds the office of director in other companies, this can sometimes be a real incentive not to dishonour a personal guarantee.

In the case of the *bank guarantee* or *performance bond*, it is common for banks and stakeholders to also require an indemnity from the party providing the funds for the issue of the guarantee or bond.

An example of the types of clauses typical of a performance bond is as follows:

    1.1   *On the occurrence of any of the following events:*

        [List of events such as breach of contract, insolvency, appointment of a receiver etc]

1.2 *The Bank* [or Stakeholder] *shall upon the written demand of X and without the necessity to ascertain or satisfy itself that the events specified in the written demand have occurred, forthwith make payment to X of the Bonded Sum or any part thereof demanded by X.*

1.3 *The obligations under this performance bond are irrevocable and shall remain in force until* _____ .

[There will also be an indemnity to the Bank/Stakeholder].

Golden Rule

Where an indemnity is required from a guarantor, it is prudent practice to obtain the indemnity as a *separate and direct obligation* from the guarantor.

So that in the event that the guarantee is unenforceable or held to be invalid for any reason, you have the comfort and protection of the indemnity directly from the party providing it.

Chapter 3

TIME AND FORM OF THE CONTRACT

■ ■ ■

Timing can be of critical importance in a contract. Often, time will be such a critical factor that adherence to deadlines will constitute the entire basis of the contract. In that event, it will be necessary to make *time of the essence* in the performance of a certain obligation or obligations.

The form of the contract becomes relevant in situations where an obligation may not have been specifically included in the contract document, or where a dispute arises concerning the existence of additional terms not expressly recorded in the contract. This can sometimes arise where a contract document does not make it clear that it records the entire agreement of the parties. Similarly, where a particular part of a contract has been held by a court to be void or unenforceable, what impact does this have upon the rest of the contract? Does it render the entire contract void?

In this chapter we will look at clauses making time an essential term of the contract, as well as understanding what an essential term actually is. We will also examine the clauses used to negative the impact of any extraneous terms not recorded in the contract and the clauses necessary to deal with a situation where an unenforceable clause can be severed from an agreement. We will also consider the question of misleading or deceptive representations in a contract and whether their effect can be minimised in any way.

■ ■ ■

Time of the essence clause

A *time of the essence* clause looks something like this:

> *Time is of the essence in* [**Party A** performing a certain action]

OR

> ***Party A*** ***shall*** [perform a certain action] *time being of the essence.*

Such wording can either stand alone or be incorporated within a longer clause dealing with the obligation to be performed.

What it is used for and why

This clause is used to make the concept of time an essential term of the contract. Firstly, it is important to understand the meaning of the expression essential term.

Golden Nugget

What is an essential term of a contract?

An essential term is a term *fundamental to the basis of the contract itself*; such that if it is not performed, alters the very nature of the contract itself.

In many jurisdictions, an essential term, once breached, gives rise to termination of the contract by the non-defaulting party. The non-defaulting party would then be entitled to sue the defaulting party for any loss suffered in respect of such termination including the concept of *loss of bargain damages*.

When using time of the essence, the concept of reasonableness is excluded. The breach of time limit by so much as a minute could mean that "all bets are off" between the parties.

Indeed the danger of making essential terms, of all time stipulations in a contract, is obvious. Every action, under a contract, which is subject to a time limit becomes an essential term, which if breached could give rise to termination of the contract and an action for damages. In any given commercial contract, that could amount to thousands of potential instances of risk.

Indeed, the danger of making essential terms of *all* time stipulations in a contract, is obvious.

Case study: painted into a corner

Effects of a "time of the essence" clause

Matt Finnisch is the Chief Executive of a large firm of painting contractors **Tucoats Pty Limited** ("**Tucoats**") providing services to the **Principal**, a large government department.

The contract involves the painting of thousands of government offices and buildings under the control of the **Principal**. The contract is an important one for **Tucoats**, as the industry is suffering from an economic downturn and painting contractors' margins are getting thinner.

During the negotiations, which were handled personally by **Matt** (on behalf of **Tucoats**), the **Principal's** lawyers insisted on making *time of the essence* for the performance of **Tucoats'** obligations under the contract. Since **Matt** did not really know what *time of the essence* actually meant (and was more concerned with concealing his uncertainty on the point), he acceded to the **Principal's** request.

One of the terms of the contract provides that **Tucoats** must perform certain painting tasks twice daily for the duration of the contract. Over the three-year term of the contract, **Tucoats** is required to perform such painting tasks a total of 2190 times (being twice-daily for three years, 365 days per year).

Remember that *time is of the essence* for the performance of such tasks by **Tucoats**. In other words, **Tucoats'** performance of its obligations — strictly on time — is an *essential term* of the contract.

This amounts to inserting 2190 essential terms into the contract, any of which, if breached, could give rise to the **Principal** potentially terminating the contract and suing **Tucoats** for damages.

The very prospect of anyone seriously demanding the inclusion of 2190 essential terms into a contract, during a negotiation, would be shouted down as unthinkable.

Yet **Matt** did not argue with the **Principal's** request to include a time of the essence clause, which would create a similar effect.

That single action — over the course of three years — constitutes 2195 separate instances which could give rise to a possible termination of the contract, in the event of a breach in any single instance. So, in the event that **Tucoats** is five minutes late on *only one* of these occasions, the **Principal** may have sufficient grounds to terminate the contract, as well as commencing legal proceedings against **Tucoats** to recover loss-of-bargain damages.

By agreeing to make time of the essence in only one contract clause, **Matt** has now exposed **Tucoats** to the risk of breaching the contract on over 2000 separate occasions — with every single occasion carrying the heavy penalty of possible contract termination.

In some jurisdictions, the effect of the time of the essence concept has been called into question and there is no clear determination. However, prudence dictates that you assume the worst and thereby, avoid trouble. Your lawyer can best advise you of the specifics of your jurisdiction and your contractual situation.

Courts may, in some circumstances, imply a time of the essence obligation to give a party a benefit that it clearly should have received. However, this is not something that should be relied upon as a substitute to good contract drafting.

■ ■

Entire agreement clause

An *entire agreement* clause looks something like this:

> *This Agreement contains the entire terms of the agreement and understanding between the parties. Each of the parties acknowledge that in entering into this Agreement on the terms set out in this Agreement it is not relying upon any representation, warranty, promise or assurance made or given by any other party or any other person, whether or not in writing, at any time prior to the execution of this Agreement which is not expressly set out in this Agreement.*

What it is used for and why

What the clause is saying — in simple terms — is that any promise made or inducement offered at any time before signing the agreement which is *not* written into the contract, has no effect.

Its effect is to prevent the parties relying upon any discussions, statements, understandings or other documents *that are not expressly embodied or contained in the contract.*

The effect of the clause is to make the contract a single "stand-alone" document containing the whole of the agreement of the parties.

Its purpose is to prevent the parties claiming — in subsequent litigation (sometimes even years after the contract was actually signed) — that the contract does not accurately reflect the agreement reached or the understanding of the parties.

However, beware that an unscrupulous individual or firm may attempt to use and rely upon the clause to their advantage, after having surreptitiously "slipped in" to the contract, any other terms not previously discussed or negotiated.

Ethically challenged organisations operating on extremely tight margins, may be tempted to engage in such practices, seeing this as the only way to make a marginal deal profitable. Such organisations tend not to rely on repeat custom when they become known for using such sharp practices.

It may also be done just to see how alert and attentive the other party is to the detail!

Regrettably, even lawyers have been known to do this to win favour with a client. Happily, however, the occurrences are few and far between.

From this, the message is that *all* successive drafts and revisions of a contract (particularly the final one to be signed) should *always* be checked thoroughly and exhaustively. Whilst the process of checking is extremely tedious and time-consuming — and therefore expensive — it must be done without fail.

The cost of failing to do so is often exponentially higher than the cost of doing it.

Golden Nugget

False and misleading representations cannot be excluded

In some jurisdictions, such a clause will be ineffective where one of the parties was induced to enter into the contract by false or misleading and deceptive representations.

In jurisdictions such as the United Kingdom, such a clause will be subject to unfair contracts legislation. Such legislation makes any contract term purporting to exclude liability for pre-contractual representations, subject to a reasonableness test. The exclusion of liability for fraudulent misrepresentation is highly unlikely to be held by a court to be reasonable.

Courts may intervene in circumstances where a contract could render actual performance to be substantially different from that which was reasonably expected.

In Australia, any such misleading and deceptive representations will fall foul of the *Trade Practices Act*. In these circumstances, where misleading and deceptive representations have been made, the *Trade Practices Act* defeats the effects of such a clause.

In many jurisdictions (including Australia), courts have held that it is not possible to use contract provisions to avoid liability under these unfair contract or trade practices statutes.

The effectiveness of entire agreement clauses will ultimately depend upon the party's approach and conduct in the negotiation of the contract and its terms (ie, by the party seeking to rely upon the clause).

In order to use the clause effectively, compliance will usually be required with the applicable laws and requirements relating to:

- unconscionable conduct;
- misleading and deceptive conduct; and
- false and misleading representations.

In light of the above, if you are a purchaser in a particular transaction and the vendor's contract includes an *entire agreement clause*, it may be wise to consider the addition of the following wording to the end of such a clause, prior to accepting it:

> *provided that this shall not exclude any liability which the Vendor would otherwise have to the Purchaser in respect of any false, misleading or fraudulent statements made by the Vendor prior to the date of this Agreement.*

Golden Nugget

Merger clause

Often in the USA and Europe, you will find the *entire agreement clause* being referred to as a *merger clause*.

The rationale for using the word *merger* to describe such a clause is that final outcome of all previous discussions and drafts is considered to be "merged" into the written document.

In other jurisdictions, such as Australia, the term *merger clause* refers to a *merger of obligations clause*, which you will see described in more detail in Chapter 5, p 111.

■ ■ ■

Further assurance clause

A *further assurance* clause may look like this:

Upon and after Completion each party shall at the request and cost of the other do and execute or procure to be done and executed all other necessary acts, deeds, documents and things within its power to give effect to the terms of this Agreement.

OR

*The Parties agree to do all acts and execute all documents necessary to give effect to the terms of this clause [**OR** to the terms of this agreement].*

What it is used for and why

Consider an example involving the purchase of a company or business. Assume the contract provides for the transfer of the entire company or business.

In such a case, there are often a multitude of things to do to give effect to the transfer as a whole. Take, for example, just some of the items one must consider (to name but a few), such as the transfer of title (ownership) in:

- owned real estate;
- copyright;
- leasehold property;
- various assets such as machinery, office equipment and motor vehicles;
- registrations such as business names;
- registrations of patents, trademarks and designs; and
- domain names.

Sometimes, a specific item that is intended to be transferred, may have been omitted. In such a case, the further assurance clause will "pick up" the omitted item to give effect to the intention of transferring the business or company as a whole.

Another way to think of the further assurance clause is a:

"If I've forgotten to specifically mention something"
clause.

Contracts do not (and cannot) provide for every eventuality and contingency. To even attempt to do so, would create telephone-directory-sized contracts for even the simplest transaction.

The further assurance clause is of use in the event that something not contemplated or foreseen by the parties creates an impediment to the intended transaction provided for by the contract.

Case study:
just in case I miss something

Let's return to the example of the purchase of the business or company referred to earlier and assume one of the motor vehicle registration certificates (in a fleet of several hundred vehicles) has been lost.

This creates an impediment to the smooth transfer of what has been purchased.

Further assume that without the registration certificate, the relevant department of transport will not register the transfer of that motor vehicle and that an additional department of transport form will also need to be completed, declaring the loss of the registration certificate.

The contract for the purchase of the business or company would unlikely have provided for this eventuality. However, the further assurance clause acts to "fill in the gaps". It allows for the orderly execution of any relevant department of transport forms, necessary to enable the transfer of the registration of the particular motor vehicle, which was sold as part of the business or company.

Other matters dealt with in such a clause

Sometimes a further assurance clause may be more detailed than the simple ones above.

Other matters that might typically be dealt with within a more elaborate form of the further assurance clause are:

- Who will bear the cost of doing further acts and executing further documents?

- Within what time limit will such acts take place?

- Will the clause operate unilaterally only?

- Is a party required to use *best endeavours* or *reasonable endeavours* in complying with the clause?

Limits of the clause

How far does the operation of the clause extend? Obviously, there is no single answer to this question. It will all depend upon the intention of the parties in the primary terms of the contract.

What is it that the parties are aiming to achieve by this contract?

For the example used, the answer to the question might be:

the parties are aiming to achieve the sale of the business or company to the purchaser and the effective transfer of all of the assets owned by the business or as described in the contract, subject to any specific exclusions within the contract.

To ascertain the limits of the clause — in the context of the particular contract — one would then read the further assurance clause with such an objective in mind.

■■■

Severance clause

A *severance* clause may look like this:

> *Each of the obligations set out in this Agreement is severable and independent so that if any clause or any part or provision of it is unenforceable then that clause or that part will be deemed eliminated or modified to the minimum extent necessary to make this Agreement or that clause or part enforceable.*

What it is used for and why

A term may turn out to be unenforceable or illegal or may subsequently become so.

A severance clause (sometimes called a *severability* clause) will attempt to sever any illegal or unenforceable term from the remaining terms without affecting the validity of those terms.

As has been mentioned above, this may be useful in preventing those provisions of an exclusion clause, which might be otherwise reasonable, from being rendered invalid by one unreasonable provision.

Where the standard terms of a company's contracts may be used in several different jurisdictions, it could be advantageous to have a clause that severs the operation of the offending clause, *only* in respect of those jurisdictions where it is illegal.

However, bear in mind that severance provisions (like any other contract provisions) are not "magic wands".

A court may decline to sever a clause, in the event that it cannot be severed without actually changing the effect of the entire agreement.

The courts seem more inclined to exercise their discretion to sever a clause when such a clause is present in an agreement. However, beware! The courts will not generally rewrite severed provisions. For example, if a court decided that a non-compete clause (or restrictive covenant) was held to be for too long a period, the court would not rewrite the clause using a shorter period. It is not the function of the courts to repair bad or incomplete contract drafting.

It is for that reason that agreements such as non-compete agreements tend to be written in the following form:

NON-COMPETE CLAUSE

X covenants with and undertakes to the Company that it will not without the prior written consent of the Company do any of the things outlined in paragraphs (a) and (b) within any of the states or territories described in paragraph (c) for the periods set out in paragraph (d) namely:

1(a) (i) *undertake, carry on or be engaged in or concerned with or interested in any business which is competitive with the Business of the Company;*

(ii) *canvass or solicit any person who or which at any time during the 12 months immediately preceding the date of termination of X's engagement is or was a client or customer of the Business;*

(iii) *canvass or solicit any employee of the Business to leave his employment with the Company;*

(iv) *counsel, procure or otherwise assist any person to do any of the acts referred to in any of the above paragraphs of this clause 1(a);*

1(b) (i) *on his own account;*

(ii) *jointly with or on behalf of any other person, firm or company;*

1(c) (i) *within New South Wales;*

(ii) *within Victoria;*

(iii) *within Queensland;*

(iv) *within Tasmania;*

(v) *within the Australian Capital Territory;*

(vi) *within South Australia;*

(vii) *within Western Australia;*

(viii) *within the Northern Territory;*

1(d) (i) *for the period ending on 1 January 2006;*

(ii) *for the period ending on 1 January 2005;*

(iii) *for the period ending on 1 January 2004;*

For example, if a court held that the inclusion of Western Australia (in 1(c)(vii)) was for some reason — unfair, it could sever that part of the agreement, without necessarily affecting the remainder of the obligation. In that case, the obligation for the person not to compete in the other states and territories would remain unaffected.

Likewise, if the period of three years (expressed in 1(d)(i)) was held to be too long a period and the provision was then severed, then the following two-year period (in 1(d)(ii)) would then be the one that remained in force.

Chapter 4

OWNERSHIP OF INFORMATION OR PROPERTY

■ ■ ■

If you agree to enter into a contractual relationship with another person it does not necessarily mean that you wish to give that other party rights of ownership to your exclusive intellectual property. Depending upon the circumstances, a measure of protection could be obtained using clauses dealing with confidentiality and secrecy. Alternatively, you might need to resort to using a retention of title clause to preserve title to an asset until you have received full payment for its sale.

Similarly, you must always take all relevant precautions to ensure that other valuable intellectual property ownership rights are not compromised or adversely affected by a contract.

You do not want to grant additional rights or even ownership through an oversight or mere inadvertence.

■■■

Retention of title (ROT) or Romalpa clause

A *retention of title* (ROT) clause — is sometimes called a *Romalpa* clause. It often looks something like this:

> *Risk of loss and damage to the goods shall pass to the Purchaser upon delivery. Title shall only pass to the Purchaser upon payment in full.*

OR a more comprehensive one might read as follows:

TITLE AND RISK

(a) *Products supplied by the Seller to the Purchaser will be at the Purchaser's risk immediately upon delivery of the Products to a recognised carrier for transport to the Purchaser or into the Purchaser's custody and control (whichever is the sooner).*

(b) *The Purchaser must:*

    (i) *effect and maintain with a reputable insurance company insurance for the Products, at its cost, against all risks as it thinks appropriate;*

    (ii) *note the interest of the Seller on the insurance policy; and*

(iii) *produce a certificate of currency of the insurance effected by the Purchaser under this clause to the Seller upon request.*

(c) *Risk in the Products will remain with the Purchaser at all times unless the Seller retakes possession of the Products in accordance with this clause.*

(d) *Title in the Products supplied by the Seller to the Purchaser will not pass to the Purchaser until those Products and any other products supplied by the Seller to the Purchaser have been paid for in full.*

(e) *Until the Products have been paid for in full:*

    (i) *the Purchaser must segregate and store the Products in such manner as to clearly indicate that they are the property of the Seller; and*

    (ii) *the Purchaser may sell the Products in the ordinary course of its business as fiduciary agent for the Seller and shall deposit the proceeds of sale (including any proceeds from insurance claims) into a separate bank account which it shall hold in trust and immediately account to the Seller therefor.*

(f) *If the Purchaser has breached these Terms and Conditions (including any payment obligations) or the terms of any relevant Sales Contract, the Purchaser authorises the Seller, at any time, to enter onto any premises upon which the Seller's Products are stored to enable the Seller to:*

    (i) *inspect the Products; and/or*

    (ii) *reclaim the Products.*

(g) *If the Purchaser sells or disposes of the Products (or part thereof) before full payment has been*

> *received by the Seller, the purchaser shall advise the Seller in writing specifying full details of the Products sold or disposed, to whom they were sold or disposed, the terms of such sale or disposal and the amount/s received or receivable by the Purchaser.*
>
> (h) *The Purchaser agrees that the provisions of this clause shall apply despite any arrangement under which the Seller grants credit to the Purchaser.*

Sometimes the ROT clause is called a Romalpa clause because in the landmark ROT case (where these issues were first explored in depth), one of the parties was called *Romalpa Aluminium Ltd*. The name has since been "adopted" by lawyers as a short-form way of saying "retention of title clause".

What it is used for and why

Under a ROT clause, the purchaser of goods takes possession of the goods but does not acquire legal title to them unless and until the goods are paid for in full.

The clause is designed to protect the seller, as it provides for the repossession of the goods, by the seller, from the purchaser who fails to pay or goes into liquidation.

The right of repossession is a very powerful right. However, what happens if the goods are no longer available on the purchaser's premises to repossess? Note that in many business situations, a purchaser of goods will typically resell those goods.

For example, a retailer of computer equipment might purchase computer systems for resale to the public.

To further complicate matters, consider a situation where that same retailer purchases individual components from various suppliers and creates its own brand of computer system, for resale. Note that it is not actually reselling the individual components in the same manner in which they were purchased. In this case, those goods are being incorporated into another product for resale.

What happens in the event of such a resale? A ROT clause usually provides that if the purchaser resells the goods, it must account to the original seller for the proceeds outstanding.

A properly drafted ROT clause should impose obligations upon the purchaser to physically segregate and specially mark stock that is subject to ROT. Furthermore, in the event of any resale, that the proceeds must be kept in a separate and specific account. In effect, the purchaser is being obliged to quarantine either stock or the proceeds from the sale of that stock.

Golden Rule

A ROT clause must be in the original contract between seller and purchaser.

To simply add it is as an afterthought, on delivery invoices, is usually not sufficient.

It is particularly interesting to note that in some jurisdictions such as Australia, courts have held that a properly drafted ROT clause actually creates a trust in favour of the original owner of the resulting proceeds of sale. In the event that the purchaser company goes into liquidation, such a trust is usually sufficient to defeat a claim brought by the liquidator on behalf of any unsecured creditors.

As an accounting note, any inventory or stock held by the purchaser company — which is the subject of a ROT provision — should not be shown on the purchaser company's balance sheet as "stock on hand", since it is not actually "owned".

Legal ownership is reserved to the original owner, pending receipt of full payment.

Case study: when the ROT sets in

How properly drafted ROT clauses protect you.

Consider the following example:

- **Smith** purchases specialised components from **Wesson**, subject to a ROT provision;

- the components purchased from **Wesson** are incorporated into products manufactured by **Smith**;

- **Smith** then sells the completed products it has produced to **Browning**, also subject to a ROT clause;
- **Browning** defaults in its payment to **Smith** and goes into liquidation.

If **Browning** has not on-sold the stock purchased from **Smith**, then a properly drafted ROT clause should enable **Smith** to actually reclaim the unsold stock.

In the event that the stock has been sold, a properly drafted ROT clause, should allow **Smith** to reclaim the proceeds of the sale of the firearms sold by **Browning** and be able to defeat the liquidator's claim.

However, **Smith** will continue to remain liable to **Wesson** for the cost of the goods, under the ROT provision in *his* contract with **Wesson**.

The wording in a ROT clause is *critical* to its success in properly protecting you. That is why your lawyer's assistance in the drafting of a suitable clause is essential. The slightest variation could render the clause ineffective.

■ ■ ■

Ownership of intellectual property clause

An *ownership of intellectual property* clause may look like this:

> *The Principal acknowledges that any and all of the Intellectual Property Rights used in connection with the Contract Works and any parts thereof are and shall remain the sole property of the Contractor or of such other party as may be identified therein or thereon (the "Owner"). In the event of any evolution of the existing Intellectual Property Rights or of any new Knowhow being generated or arising from the performance of or as a result of the Contract Works, the Principal hereby acknowledges that the same and all Intellectual Property Rights therein shall belong to the Contractor exclusively unless otherwise agreed in writing by an Authorised Officer of the Contractor.*

What it is used for and why

Often, one party will "bring to the table" some form of proprietary information, product or other expertise. Depending upon the circumstances, this can actually be one of the prime reasons behind the Contractor's ultimate selection by a Principal. This category of intellectual property rights may sometimes be referred to as *background intellectual property rights.*

The intellectual property rights created during the course of a contract are sometimes referred to as *foreground intellectual property rights.*

A Contractor will generally seek to retain both categories of rights.

It will depend upon the particular circumstances of the situation whether:

- the Principal is paying the Contractor only for some *limited right to use* such proprietary information; or

- the Principal is paying the Contractor to actually devise or develop such proprietary information for the Principal's exclusive use and ownership.

This is a crucial point to bear in mind. It is something that must be absolutely clear and unequivocal in the contract documentation.

Depending upon the circumstances, the Principal's contract documents may contain provisions either granting the Principal the exclusive ownership of the intellectual property developed by the Contractor or perhaps only granting some form of limited permission for its use. A Principal must be aware that it may be prevented from accessing such intellectual property after termination of the contract. Such an arrangement could effectively tie-up the Principal for many years.

Moral rights

Note that the concept of *moral rights* exists in some jurisdictions. The moral rights of an author of literary, dramatic, musical or artistic works and cinematograph films are enshrined in legislation in some jurisdictions such as New South Wales. A moral right generally refers to a right of attribution of authorship or a right of integrity of authorship.

Whilst infringement is not usually an offence under the legislation, it does give rise to a right of action by the author for infringement. Remedies for infringement of moral rights could include:

- the issue of an injunction;

- an award of damages for loss resulting from the infringement;

- a declaration that a moral right of the author has been infringed;

- an order that the defendant make a public apology for the infringement; or

- an order that any false attribution of authorship be removed or reversed.

Your lawyer will be able to best advise you on the necessary safeguards, if your situation has the potential to fall into this category.

Third party claims

When dealing with intellectual property issues, it is common (and not unreasonable) for a Principal to seek protection (usually in the form of an indemnity clause) against claims by any third party that:

- the intellectual property claimed to be owned by the Contractor infringes some right of the third party; or

- the use of such intellectual property by the Principal constitutes an infringement of such third party's rights.

In such cases, the Principal is attempting to verify the Contractor's clear ownership and title to the items that the Principal is contracting for the Contractor to supply.

Case study: it's mine!

What happens when you need to use another's proprietary information

Consider the situation where **Phil Anderer** ("**Phil**") provides certain specialised services to a large national chain of introduction agencies called **Matchem and Despatchem (Matchem)**.

As part of these services, **Phil** is to develop specialised and innovative computer software to enable the management of **Matchem's** data in a much more streamlined and cost-effective fashion. **Matchem's** data is critical to it and **Matchem** cannot afford to lose the data or any functionality with the systems that manage and manipulate such data.

The contract between them contains the following clause:

PROPRIETARY RIGHTS.

*Notwithstanding anything contained herein to the contrary, the Contractor (**Phil**) shall retain all title, copyright, patent and other proprietary rights to all Contractor-developed or owned computer programs, modules, software, products, designs, methodology, analytical processes, computer equipment, data record forms, procedures, internal reports and forms used, created or developed by the Contractor in the performance of its services hereunder.*

*All data supplied by the Principal (**Matchem**) shall be and remain at all times the sole and exclusive property of the Principal.*

Notice the clause contains:

- a statement of ownership by the Contractor of the intellectual property; and

- a statement of ownership by the Principal of all the data supplied by it.

However, the clause does not deal with what are, in fact, the most crucial questions for **Matchem**:

- What happens *after* termination or expiration of the contract?

- How will the Principal be able to access and manipulate its data?

- Will the data created or generated on the Contractor's system be compatible with the Principal's system?

For **Matchem**, the continuity and integrity of its data is vital to its survival. To this end, the contract between them should contain an obligation upon the Contractor to either:

- licence its software to **Matchem**, for an established fee, to enable it to access, view and manipulate the data; and/or

- to create an appropriate and fully functioning interface, which will enable **Matchem** to view, manipulate and integrate all of the data (including data generated or created by the Contractor's system during the term of the contract) with **Matchem's** existing system.

In addition, there should also be *continuing* obligations to provide for the Contractor's technical and other support, necessary to provide the functionality required to give effect to such obligations.

It can be seen that the initial clause above is critically lacking in this regard. Consequently, **Matchem** runs a grave risk of having years of data compiled without the ability to effectively access, read and manipulate such data in the future.

It is important that sufficient time and attention be devoted to these issues from the outset to avoid uncertainty for the future and to also avoid being in the situation where **Matchem** could be held "to ransom" for its vital data by an unscrupulous **Phil Anderer**.

■■■

Confidentiality clause

A *confidentiality* clause often looks something like this:

1. *The Vendor and Purchaser shall keep confidential:*
   (a) *all information exchanged between them during discussions and negotiations preceding this contract;*
   (b) *all information exchanged between them pursuant to this contract; and*
   (c) *the terms of this contract*

   and will cause all persons employed by and associated with them to also keep same confidential.

To the above clause, it is appropriate and usual to allow certain prescribed and defined exceptions to permit specified disclosures to be made.

Note that it is best to be as specific as possible in allowing such exceptions:

2. *The Vendor and the Purchaser may make such disclosures in relation to the information referred to in clause 1 above and this contract:*

   (a) *to employees, legal advisers, financial advisers, auditors and other consultants of the relevant Party or its related bodies corporate requiring the information for the purposes of this contract;*

   (b) *where the relevant Party who supplied the information has first granted its express written consent to do so;*

   (c) *if the information is, as at the date this contract is entered into* **[optional but useful]**, *lawfully in the possession of the recipient of the information through sources other than the Party who supplied the information and there is no obligation to keep the information confidential;*

   (d) *if the information is generally and publicly available other than as a result of breach of confidence by the person receiving the information.*

With publicly listed corporations, stock exchange listing requirements mandate the making of such public announcements for certain events. In other situations, there may need to be notifications to a competition regulator. To cover such eventualities, the following should be added to the above:

> (e) *if required by law, by any competent governmental authority or the rules of a recognised stock exchange;*

> 3. *A Party disclosing information under clause 2 must use [**best** OR **all reasonable**] endeavours to ensure that persons receiving confidential information from it do not disclose the information except in the circumstances permitted in this clause.*

On certain occasions and in certain transactions, parties will need to issue a press release announcing the particular transaction. In such cases, it might be wise to consider the following additional clause:

> 4. *Notwithstanding clauses 1, 2 and 3, the parties may agree to the release of certain information deemed confidential by this contract by way of press release. No such information shall be released under this clause unless both the vendor and the purchaser have expressly agreed to the content and timing of the press release.*

It is usually good practice to add a merger clause attaching to a confidentiality obligation, to ensure this clause "survives" after completion of the contract.

5. *This **clause** does not merge on completion.*

See **Merger of obligations clause** in Chapter 5, p 111, for more information on this point.

What it is used for and why

Most companies have information they regard as valuable and commercially sensitive. For example, they may possess specialised know-how and processes, customer information or lists, research and development, financial and other commercial data.

Contracts that parties enter into generally contain sensitive information about pricing and margins, which a particular party (or all of the parties) will wish to keep confidential from the public.

As a result, they need to safeguard such information to ensure that it does not fall into the hands of competitors or potential competitors, who might then be in a position to exploit such information to the detriment of the party to which it belongs.

Organisations and individuals need to be certain commercially sensitive information passed to other parties, in a transaction, will only be used for a limited and specified purpose. A confidentiality clause is usually the best method to prevent the improper use of information by the party receiving the information and thereby gaining or exploiting an unfair advantage, through the use of such information.

In certain situations, it may be appropriate and necessary for a confidentiality agreement to be entered into before any discussions take place that may ultimately lead to a contract being signed.

■ ■ ■

Exclusivity provisions

An exclusivity provision is designed to "lock-in" a period during which the Discloser (**A**) of confidential information cannot enter into a contract with any other party during the exclusivity period.

It often looks something like this:

A grants B an exclusive right to purchase X until 31st December 2003 on purchase terms ultimately acceptable to A.

A agrees, to the extent permitted by law, on its own behalf and on behalf of its related bodies corporate that they will not (and will procure that its advisors will not) from the date of execution of this agreement until 31st December 2003 enter into any agreement to sell X to any party other than B:

To broaden the concept and to further strengthen the exclusivity provision, it might be appropriate for the clause to provide that the Discloser (A) shall not provide any information to or hold any discussions with any other party during the exclusivity period.

A grants B an exclusive right to purchase X until 31st December 2003 on purchase terms ultimately acceptable to A.

A agrees, to the extent permitted by law, on its own behalf and on behalf of its related bodies corporate that they will not (and will procure that its advisors will not) from the date of execution of this agreement until 31st December 2003:

(a) *enter into any agreement to sell X to any party other than B;*

(b) *approach or solicit enquiries from, or initiate discussions with any new third party in relation to a proposal to dispose of X; or*

(c) *participate in any discussions or negotiations with, or provide any information to, any third party in connection with the proposed sale of X;*

(d) *allow any party other than B to conduct due diligence;*

(e) *disclose the existence or contents of this letter or the fact that discussions with B are taking place in connection with the proposed sale of X.*

What it is used for and why

The typical reason for requesting an exclusivity provision is where the Recipient of confidential information is about to embark on an expensive investigation exercise (such as a *due diligence* on the acquisition of a business) prior to making a firm commitment (executing a contract) to proceed with a transaction.

Because of the time required and the expense needed to be outlaid for the process, the Recipient will want to be certain that those monies expended will not be wasted because the "rug was pulled from under them", by the Discloser selling the business to another party before the Recipient had concluded its investigations and had the opportunity to make a final decision.

When asked by the Recipient to include an exclusivity provision in an agreement, it may be appropriate, in some circumstances, to require that a *break-fee* provision be included. A *break-fee*, typically, is a non-refundable payment to be made to the Discloser by the Recipient of confidential information, in the event that the Recipient does not proceed with the transaction, after the expiration of the exclusivity period.

The *break-fee* concept may help determine whether a Recipient is serious in its intentions and that its request for exclusivity is a genuine one, or whether the exclusivity request is merely indiscriminate and purely designed to create a tactical delay for the Discloser; for example, by keeping a business the Discloser is trying to sell "off the market", for the duration of the exclusivity period.

■ ■ ■

Non-solicitation provision
(sometimes called an anti-poaching provision)

This is often one of the most sensitive and valuable issues to a Discloser of confidential information. A Discloser does not want a Recipient to capitalise (to the detriment of the Discloser) upon knowledge of customer or supplier lists and details of key employees. This is particularly so where the Recipient is a direct competitor of the Discloser.

Often exceptions are included in such clauses where the solicitation occurs purely coincidentally, (in a large company for example) and that such persons engaged in the solicitation of an employee, have no knowledge of the confidential information.

Exceptions are also common dealing with instances where an employee voluntarily responds to a publicly placed job advertisement.

For a more comprehensive discussion on confidentiality agreements as well as seeing specific examples of the use of such documents, you should consult the second volume in the *Commercial Contracts for Managers Series* titled ***Understanding Confidentiality Agreements***.

Chapter 5

PERFORMANCE ISSUES

███

There are a number of situations that can arise during the performance of the contract that will require certain actions to be performed by one or more parties. For example, a properly drawn contract will set out the actions required to be followed and the approvals necessary to be obtained, where one of the contracting parties is sold. Or, it may be as simple as defining the steps necessary for the proper services of a notice upon the other party.

In addition, in certain circumstances, a contract might ideally contain provisions governing the manner in which a power and/or discretion vested in one of the parties is exercised.

Certain administrative actions, such as setting-off a payment *owing by a party* against monies *owed to that party* are also dealt with in this chapter.

■ ■ ■

Obligation to act reasonably

An *obligation to act reasonably* clause often looks like this:

> *Wherever the Principal or Contract Administrator is required to make any decision or determination, give any direction, exercise any discretion, form any opinion, give any interpretation or exercise any powers, it shall at all times act reasonably and do so upon reasonable grounds*

OR

> *Where any reference is made in this Contract to:*
>
> a) *Times, time limits or periods in any notices issued to the Contractor;*
>
> b) *Costs incurred by the Principal;*
>
> c) *Grounds for the making of any decision or determination by the Principal or the Contract Administrator;*
>
> d) *Any actions of the Principal or the Contract Administrator;*
>
> e) *The giving of any direction by the Principal or the Contract Administrator;*
>
> f) *The exercise of any discretion by the Principal or the Contract Administrator;*
>
> g) *Where the Principal or the Contract Administrator is required to form any opinion;*

h) *Where the Principal or the Contract Administrator is required to give any interpretation;*

i) *Where the Principal or the Contract Administrator is required to exercise any powers;*

they shall at all times be reasonable and made or given upon reasonable grounds.

What it is used for and why

In the United States of America, it is common for contracts to expressly impose an obligation of good faith and fair dealing upon the parties to that contract.

In the absence of a special relationship — such as that of employer–employee or insurer–insured — in most jurisdictions, there appears to be no general obligation in contract law for arm's-length commercial parties to a contract, to act reasonably. In some jurisdictions, however, this duty may be implied.

The question remains, what does it mean to act "reasonably"? A typical lawyer's answer would be that it depends on the circumstances. A cynic might suggest it is "whatever you can get away with" without breaching a contract or being accused of being fraudulent. Assume there are two parties to a contract: the Contractor providing a particular service or services to the Principal. To overcome any doubts, the inclusion into a contract of the *obligation to act reasonably* clause similar to the one above, can be a useful tool in some circumstances.

In many contracts, especially government contracts, the contracts' administrator (representing the Principal) has very wide and extensive powers. On occasion, the personality of the contract administrator can have a substantial effect on the working relationship with the Contractor and in extreme cases, perhaps also on the Contractor's profitability.

It would be prudent to request the inclusion of such a clause to apply not just to a single instance where the Principal is making a decision or exercising a discretion, but to the *whole* of the contract.

You would do well to assume that a court in your jurisdiction would not be prepared to imply any obligation to act reasonably in relation to a Principal's exercise of any powers conferred by the contract. In jurisdictions where the duty is not implied, a court will consider that such a duty is not necessary for the proper commercial operation of the contract.

Good faith

A slight variation on the *obligation to act reasonably* is the obligation to exercise good faith, as set out in the following clause:

> ### GOOD FAITH
>
> *In the event that any matter arises, in the course of carrying out the transactions set forth in or contemplated by this Agreement, for which no (or no adequate) provision has been made in this Agreement, the parties shall negotiate in good faith and agree on any necessary amendments to this Agreement.*

Golden Rule

If you require the other party to your contract to act reasonably in its dealings with you, it is good practice to expressly state this in your contract.

■ ■ ■

Waiver clause

A *waiver* clause may look like this:

> *In no event shall any delay, failure or omission on the part of either of the parties in enforcing exercising or pursuing any right, power, privilege,*

claim or remedy, which is conferred by this Agreement, or arises under this Agreement, or arises from any breach by any of the other parties to this Agreement of any of its obligations hereunder, be deemed to be or be construed as:

(i)   *a waiver thereof, or of any other such right power privilege claim or remedy, in respect of the particular circumstances in question; or*

(ii) *operate so as to bar the enforcement or exercise thereof, or of any other such right, power, privilege, claim or remedy, in any other instance at any time or times thereafter.*

What it is used for and why

In many jurisdictions, a failure by a party to exercise its rights (or even to exercise them punctually) can, in some circumstances, constitute a *waiver* of those rights.

In some jurisdictions, the legal terms used are *laches* or *acquiescence*. That is, since one party has elected not to exercise its rights, it is said to have *acquiesced* to the conduct of the other. In this way that party has effectively surrendered such rights.

For this reason, it is necessary to have a safeguard in the event that one chooses not to enforce existing rights, for the time being, by reason of:

- inadvertence or oversight ("we just didn't get around to it"); or

- the commercial realities of a situation (such as the maintenance of an important strategic relationship).

A clause is needed to provide that a party's waiver of a breach on one occasion will not affect its rights to enforce, if there is a further breach or if it requires compliance at a later time.

The clause shown above operates in favour of all parties to the agreement. However, it is common to see it operating only unilaterally in favour of one of the parties to the agreement; usually the party responsible for the drafting of the contract. For example, the clause will usually operate in favour of the vendor in a sale and purchase situation.

In some circumstances, it may be appropriate, to request that such a clause operate in favour of all parties.

It is important when considering waiver clauses, that they be of a practical nature, to accommodate the typical ebbs and flows of business relationships, whilst continuing to operate as a safeguard in the preservation of rights.

Some features to bear in mind when considering waiver clauses are:

- **A waiver of a provision in a contract or of a right should be binding upon the party granting the waiver only if it is given in writing and is signed by the authorised officer of the party granting the waiver.**

  This avoids a situation arising such as *"Fred told me it was OK"*.

- **A waiver should only be effective in the *specific instance* and *for the specific purpose* for which it is given.**

  You do not want a waiver that you had given in one situation, to be used against you in totally different circumstances.

- **A single or partial exercise of a right by a party does not preclude another exercise or attempted exercise of that right or the exercise of another right.**

  AND

- **Failure by a party to exercise or delay in exercising a right does not prevent its exercise or operate as a waiver.**

  These last two points are helpful, particularly in instances where indulgences might sometimes be extended to the other party when trying to maintain a particularly unsteady commercial relationship — which subsequently breaks down. In that event, you still wish to retain all of your contractual rights to be able to enforce, either offensively or defensively.

■ ■ ■

Assignment clause

An *assignment* clause may look like this:

> *A party must not transfer, assign, create an interest in or deal in any other way with any of its rights under this Agreement without the prior written consent of the other party.*

OR

> *A party must not transfer, assign, create an interest in or deal in any other way with any of its rights under this Agreement without the prior written consent of the other parties which consent shall not be unreasonably withheld or delayed.*

What it is used for and why

An assignment clause (for the purposes of this section) is quite simply a transfer of rights, benefits and obligations under a contract from one party (called the *assignor*) to another party (called the *assignee*).

Parties often go to great lengths to select other parties prior to entering into a contract relationship with them. They apply a number of criteria judged to be important to ultimately select the other party they believe best fulfils such criteria. After such a rigorous process, a party will usually wish to ensure that it continues to deal with the entity it had selected.

Many will usually require the option of terminating the contract in the event of any attempt at substituting the other party or in the event of a *change of control* in the other party's company (see also **Change of control clause**, p 106). At the very least, many would find it desirable to have a process to have the final right of approval of any change in the other party.

Parties, therefore, tend to agree on the benefits of having an assignment clause in their contract, containing specified conditions restricting and governing the assignment of the one party's interest in the contract to another party. The assignment clause will usually contain a restriction preventing any assignment of such interest without the other's written consent. The primary reason being that another party proposing to take the place of the assignor will often be unknown to the other party.

In many contractual relationships, one of the parties tends to have the "upper hand" over the other. For example, in a tendering situation, the Principal will usually have the upper hand over the Contractor. In these situations, assignment clauses can often operate unilaterally preventing the tenderer from assigning whilst expressly permitting the Principal to assign its interest at will and without the necessity of requiring the other party's approval.

In such a situation where an assignment clause permits a Contractor to assign its interest, it will be common for there to be certain conditions allowing a Principal to withhold consent to the assignment until:

☑ **certain conditions prescribed by the assignment clause are satisfied by the Contractor;**

For example, the Principal may wish to withhold consent until the existing breaches of the agreement by the Contractor have been remedied.

☑ **the steps prescribed by the assignment clause have been followed by the Contractor (and the incoming party) and;**

For example, the Contractor may have to follow certain steps regarding the form and timing of notice to the Principal of the proposed assignment. Also regarding the timely provision of relevant information requested by the Principal.

☑ **certain criteria prescribed by the assignment clause have been met by the incoming party.**

For example, the new Contractor may have to establish proof of their reputation, financial strength and stability, a particular type of insurance coverage, trade or bank references, demonstrated skills to be able to perform certain specialised tasks etc. These criteria must be satisfied by the new Contractor to a standard that is no less favourable to the Principal.

■ ■ ■

Change of control clause

A change of control clause often looks like this:

Change of Control

(a) *In the event of a Change of Control in respect of any party the following provisions shall apply:*

(b) *"Change of Control" for the purposes of this clause means any of the following:*

    (i) *transfers or allotments of shares in the capital of any Party (or a Parent of any Party) which have the effect of altering the identity of the person or group of persons who held 51% of the capital of that Party (or a Parent of that Party) immediately prior to such transfer or allotment; or*

    (ii) *an alteration in the composition of the board of directors or other committee organ or decision making forum of any Party (or a Parent of any Party) which results in the persons who exercised management control over the business and affairs of that Party (or a Parent of that Party) prior to such change ceasing to exercise such control, but does not include any such transfer, allotment or alteration where the ultimate shareholding in or control of (whichever is applicable) the relevant Party remains unaltered by such transfer, allotment or alteration.*

(c) *The Party affected by a Change of Control must immediately notify the other Parties in writing of that fact and supply all relevant material particulars of the Change of Control to the other parties.*

(d) *Upon a Change of Control the other Parties shall, for a period of 30 Business Days after the date of receipt of notification thereof from the affected party, be entitled to ...*

What it is used for and why

A useful supplement to an assignment clause is the *change of control* clause. This clause governs the situation where there is a change in the ownership or control of a party to the contract.

A change of control clause will generally define the events constituting a change of control. It will provide that any change of control (that falls within such definition) will:

• trigger a certain set of events such as termination; or

- may be *deemed* to be an assignment. Such a deeming provision will then trigger the same information and approval processes necessary in an assignment situation.

One way of broadening the change of control clause is to define one of the events constituting a change of control to be any change in the *effective* control of the company. This caters for situations where an event does not constitute a change in the *legal or ownership* control of the company, but in reality does create a change of *actual* control.

Examples of such an event could be:

- the appointment or removal of all (or the majority) of the directors or other equivalent officers of the Contractor; or

- giving directions with respect to the operating and financial policies of the Contractor, which the directors or other equivalent officers of the Contractor are obliged to comply with.

To further broaden its scope, the change of control clause should also extend to dealing with any change of control over the *parent company* of any party to the contract.

It is not unheard of for a company that was unsuccessful in securing a particular contract to seek to acquire the company that is a party to the contract. In this way, it thereby secures the contract "through the back door".

This would be especially likely where such a contract carried a considerable financial or strategic significance to the acquirer.

■ ■ ■

Service of notices

One of the formalities of any agreement is to provide for the proper services of notices to the parties to the agreement.

Notices not conforming to the protocol outlined in the *services of notices* provision could be deemed to have been given much later than was actually the case, or in a worst case scenario, not to have *ever* been given. This could have disastrous consequences in the event that the notice was a particularly crucial one such as a termination notice or price increase notice.

Notices are given either to trigger, or because of, important or significant events in a contract. For this reason, it is important that the service of notices provision be scrutinised carefully to ensure that it is *practically* workable and effective. For example, in a contract between parties in separate countries, a provision specifying that *all* notices could only be hand-delivered by a director of one party to a director of the other party, would be impractical, expensive and unworkable.

A typical clause will usually provide for:

- the name of the representative of the party and the address at which any notice must be served;

- the method of service; and

- circumstances in which a notice is deemed to have been served.

The following example clause relates to an agreement between parties in different countries. Hence, the specification of airmail (as the postal service method), the ten-day postal service period, and the language of the notice. Such matters would not be typically included where the parties and the subject matter of the contract all reside within the same jurisdiction.

Notices

1.1 *All written notices between the parties required or permitted under this Agreement shall be:*

    i.   *in writing; and*

    ii. *sent to the other party's address as shown below; and*

    iii. *legible;*

    iv. *in the English language; and*

    v. *delivered by prepaid registered airmail post with return receipt, or sent by facsimile transmission.*

1.2 *The respective addresses for service of any notices upon the parties are as follows:*

[INSERT NAMES, FULL ADDRESSES AND FAX NUMBERS OF EACH PARTY TO THE CONTRACT (INCLDING ANY GUARANTORS)]

1.3 *Any such notice shall be deemed effectively given:*

(i) *if by facsimile, upon receipt by the sender of the printed facsimile confirmation receipt following transmission; and*

(ii) *if by mail, ten days after such communication was actually sent.*

1.4 *Each party shall notify any other party to this Agreement of any change to its name, relevant addressee, address or fax number in accordance with this clause.*

■ ■ ■

Merger of obligations clause

This clause ensures that parties to a contract continue to be responsible to carry out certain obligations under the contract, even after completion of the transaction.

The words used tend to be along the following lines:

Clauses 1, 2 and 3 shall not merge on completion.

The clause should nominate the specific clauses intended to continue to be in force and have effect, *after* completion.

What it is used for an why

Where a clause is specified to *not merge on completion*, the rights and obligations conferred by the clause it refers to "survive" and continue to be in force *after* completion of the contractual transaction.

Arguably such a clause overlaps to some extent with the general law of many jurisdictions.

Under the general law, rights which were intended by the parties to continue after completion, will do so.

These generally tend to be rights that are required to continue even after the main subject matter of a contract is completed. For example, in the case of a sale of an object, the contract is completed once the purchaser pays the purchase price and takes possession of the object. However, some rights will need to continue unaffected by the completion of the sale. Some of these rights tend to be the following:

- confidentiality;
- non-solicitation or non-competition;
- warranties;

- indemnities; and

- guarantees.

Notwithstanding that, in many cases, a merger clause may be a restatement of the general law, it is often a useful reminder to the parties.

In the USA and in Europe, the term *merger clause* actually refers to an *entire agreement clause*. The rationale for using the word *merger* to describe such a clause is that the final outcome of all previous discussions and drafts is considered to be "merged" into the written document. In Chapter 3, p 59 you will see a description of the *entire agreement clause*.

Sometimes, you may see a "blanket" merger clause stating that all clauses in the agreement survive completion. It is often expressed along the following lines:

> *The provisions of this Agreement are capable of having effect after completion of any transaction referred to herein and do not merge on completion of any transaction referred to herein.*

However, the use of such a blanket clause is not "best practice" contract drafting. For example, in an agreement for the sale of an object, it would be nonsensical to suggest that an obligation to pay the purchase price survives completion, if the purchase price has already been paid.

However, as a counter to such an argument, one might consider the use of one of the following forms of clause:

The provisions of this Agreement shall not merge insofar as they have not been fulfilled at the time of completion.

OR

To the extent that any obligation contained within this Agreement has not been fulfilled prior to completion, such obligation shall not merge and shall continue to have full force and effect.

■ ■ ■

Variations to the contract

It should go without saying, but it is useful to restate it anyway, that all variations, amendments to or departures from the contract document must be in writing and signed by the parties.

This eliminates the situation, in the face of an obvious breach of contract by the other party, of you being told that:

Joe from your office said it would be OK.

A typical *variations* clause reads as follows:

Variation
A variation of any term of this Agreement must be in writing and signed by the parties.

■■■

Set-off clause

A typical set-off clause might look something like this:

> *The Principal is entitled, but not obliged, at any time to set off any liability of the Contractor to the Principal against any liability of the Principal to the Contractor (howsoever arising in either case). Any exercise by the Principal of its rights under this clause shall be without prejudice to any other rights entitlements or remedies available to the Principal against the Contractor.*

What it is used for and why

The right of set-off is typically relevant where two parties have mutual liabilities to one another. The mutual liabilities need not be for the same amounts or even arising from the same transaction. Consider a situation where:

- **Wolfe** owes **Fox** $50;

- at the same time, **Wolfe** is owed $100 by **Fox**.

In the absence of any right of set-off existing, as *two separate transactions* **Wolfe** is obliged to:

- pay **Fox** the $50 that **Wolfe** owes; and

- separately attempt to collect from **Fox** the $100 that is owed by **Fox**.

As the scenario above demonstrates, the right of set-off can be a great administrative convenience, as well as a safeguard; where someone owes you money, you can set-off their indebtedness against any monies you might owe to them.

Administratively, it prevents duplication of efforts — where the same parties involved — in paying an amount *owing by you* to one party and then having to separately collect an amount *owed to you* by that same party. As a safeguard, it can be a valuable advantage where you may be experiencing difficulties in recovering monies owed to you by a party, especially where you have the luxury of being able to set-off such amounts against monies owing by you to that recalcitrant party.

In a typical money-lending situation, the bank will be entitled to set-off the balance of any savings you have on deposit with the bank against any amounts owed by you to the bank under a loan. For any bank, this represents a sure-fire and effective means of settling a debt (or part thereof) owed by a customer, with a simple book entry.

This, in essence, explains the raison d'être of the set-off clause.

Chapter 6

JURISDICTIONAL ISSUES

■ ■ ■

Some of the most fundamental and important selections to be made in any contract are the choices of:

- *law* applicable to the contract;

- the relevant *court* that might be called upon to interpret any of the contractual provisions, in the event of a dispute arising between the parties; and

- *language* in which the official version of the contract is to be written. What value (if any) will any translations of that document have?

These are serious choices that can have a major impact on the effect of the contract and the cost of resolving any disputes that might eventually arise.

■■■

Governing law and jurisdiction clause

A governing law and jurisdiction clause often looks like this:

> *This agreement is governed by the laws of California. The parties agree to submit to the* [**exclusive** or **non-exclusive**] *jurisdiction of the courts of California for the settlement or adjudication of any disputes arising out of this agreement.*

OR

> *This Agreement together with any document executed pursuant to it (save as may be provided for therein) shall be governed by and construed in accordance with the laws of New South Wales, Australia. Each party irrevocably and unconditionally:*
>
> a) *submits to the* [**exclusive** or **non-exclusive**] *jurisdiction of the courts of New South Wales; and*
>
> b) *waives any and all claim or objection based on absence of jurisdiction or inconvenient forum.*

What it is used for and why

In the event of any dispute or call for interpretation of the contents of the document, it is necessary to have a statement of the applicable law governing the document. The parties will need to agree upon the law of a particular place, which will govern the interpretation of the contract.

It is usually accompanied by a statement of the jurisdiction, specifying the applicable jurisdiction or *forum* (place) for the settlement of any disputes arising. That is, which courts (of a particular state or country) are empowered to hear and adjudicate upon, any disputes arising from the contract. For example, such a statement will specifically declare the contract to be "governed by and interpreted under the laws of Japan", with the courts of that country having jurisdiction.

The party with the conduct of the drafting of the contract will (naturally enough) tend to choose its own local law and jurisdiction, where possible.

When considering the structure of a contract from the logical perspective of the layperson, one would think that this would be the *first* item that needs to be agreed upon. However, in practice it is often one of the *last*, or more incidental issues to be determined.

However, its importance should not be discounted — as it can have an enormous impact on the cost of any subsequent litigation. Litigation can be an expensive enough proposition when it occurs domestically. The situation exponentially worsens when having to fly and accommodate lawyers, managers and staff abroad for the process. Legal costs often double as two sets of lawyers are employed for the task (one set in the "home" jurisdiction and one abroad).

Debates over the determination of which jurisdiction to adopt in the contract usually centre on the *physical* location of the parties and, more particularly, *the location of the subject matter of the contract*. That is, the location where the terms of the contract are actually being carried out.

In the case of the performance of a singular service in a particular location, the task of reaching agreement on an appropriate jurisdiction can be a relatively easy one.

However, the task becomes more complicated where parties from different countries are performing services in a number of other countries. Consider a situation where, as an example, a US firm ("USCO") contract with a company based in the Netherlands ("**Dutchco**"). **USCO** performs a service (or supplies goods) to **Dutchco's** subsidiaries throughout Europe, in multiple locations.

The most appropriate jurisdiction will be determined by negotiation between them and incorporated into the terms of the Master Supply Agreement between **Dutchco** and **USCO**.

If the purchaser of the services (**Dutchco**) is in a stronger bargaining position, it may have the advantage of securing the applicable law and jurisdiction as its own — in such case, **USCO** might wish the jurisdiction to be specified as "non-exclusive".

■■■

Jurisdiction — "exclusive" or "non-exclusive"?

The selection of a *non-exclusive* jurisdiction clause could be a "double-edged sword", in that it may allow an opposing party that same flexibility to choose an alternative venue. This may not always be a desirable proposition.

In some instances, a degree of flexibility in choosing an appropriate jurisdiction is not required by the party drawing the contract, such as in the instance of the sale of a company or a business:

- A vendor is unlikely to need to sue anybody.
  The vendor's primary concern in the transaction is obtaining payment from the purchaser. If it is not paid, it does not complete the transaction. In such transactions, it invariably tends to be the purchaser that initiates legal action.

- In the event of the vendor ever needing to initiate litigation, it would generally be in the vendor's home territory. There is usually no reason why it would want to do so anywhere else.

Some lawyers express the view that by making a jurisdiction clause too restrictive (ie, by choosing *exclusive* jurisdiction), they may make it easier for the other party to strike-down such a clause.

Other lawyers are of the view that it makes little difference whether the jurisdiction selected is *exclusive* or *non-exclusive*. This is because of the degree of difficulty, in practice, of transferring proceedings away from a nominated non-exclusive jurisdiction. English courts would appear willing to do so only in "an extreme situation".

However, given the conflicting views, the maximum degree of certainty would appear to be obtained with the use of an *exclusive* jurisdiction clause.

■ ■ ■

Language clause

A *language* clause may look like this:

> *This agreement is drawn up in the English language. Any translation of the document into another language is for the convenience of the parties only and such translations will not have the force of law. The English language text of the document shall prevail over any other.*

What it is used for and why

Often if the parties are in different countries several language versions of the document may end up in circulation.

Only one of the versions will be the "original" language version of the document. The effect of this will be to give the original language version precedence over all others for the purposes of interpretation. Translations are usually expressly relegated to items of convenience only, with no binding effect upon the parties.

Often, the *prevailing language* clause accompanies (and should be consistent with) the governing law and jurisdiction clauses.

Otherwise, you could be faced with the incongruous (and monstrously expensive) prospect of the parties in a contract dispute over a document in the Swedish language using the governing law of the Netherlands in an Australian court! This is not as far fetched as it sounds, as I have actually seen it happen in a contract between two large multinational corporations. The end result is likely to be complicated in a number of ways.

Significantly, the language of the document is likely to be foreign to at least one of the parties. Sometimes, the language can be foreign to *both* parties; for example, where a *French* and an *Italian* company are entering into a contract written in the *English* language.

There is always potential for additional complications and misunderstandings to arise when translations are incorrect (and despite the best intentions and exhaustive efforts of the parties, they often can be).

There was once a presentation by a well-known insurance broker (through an interpreter) to a group of senior executives, in another country, concerning the benefits of *captive* insurance companies. The group sat stony-faced for two hours and abruptly left the presentation at its conclusion, without concluding any business or even asking a single question. It was not until much later that the broker discovered that the interpreter had translated *captive* insurance company as *prisoner* insurance company to the executives. The dumbfounded executives had no idea what on earth prisoner insurance companies were and why they would ever wish to do business with prisoners.

When it comes to language, the level of proficiency (at a business level), of the contracting company's staff, in a second language, can sometimes be severely limited or even non-existent. When this occurs, it is a potential recipe for trouble or even disaster, in a worst-case scenario.

Golden Rule

Bear in mind that in some countries (for example, in Saudi Arabia), their local law will *impose* the local language of that country as the prevailing language, whenever the contract is expressed to be subject to the law of that country.

That is why it is important to have expert legal advice, particularly so, in cross-border transactions, as there may be local law traps that may not have been anticipated or foreseen.

Chapter 7

DAMAGES, DISPUTES AND TERMINATION

■ ■ ■

This is where "the rubber meets the road". The test of any contract is how it stands up to scrutiny under a number of bright lights.

When things turn sour, this is the first place in the contract to which the parties will be turning. The first discussions with lawyers will invariably be concerning these clauses.

Some of the clauses in this chapter are used to regulate the manner in which parties settle their disputes. Another category of clauses are concerned with the method of calculating damages or even deciding in which situations monetary damages (on their own) would not offer sufficient protection to the party. One other category of clauses are those used to apportion liability between parties or to outsource liability to another party or parties.

Some clauses are used to regulate the method the parties agree to adopt upon termination of the contract. Often, if this is done within a tightly regulated and pre-agreed scheme, the potential for disagreement and acrimony is significantly reduced.

■■■

Liquidated damages clause

A typical *liquidated damages* clause reads along the following lines:

> *In the event that delivery is delayed for any reason (other than a Force Majeure Event) the Vendor shall pay as liquidated and ascertained damages to the Purchaser a sum calculated at the rate of* **[for example, one half of one per cent (0.5%)]** *of the Contract Price of the goods actually delayed for each Business Day between the delivery date stipulated in the Contract for the relevant goods and the actual date of their delivery up to a maximum of* **[for example, seven per cent (7%)]** *of the Contract Price.*

What it is used for and why

On occasion, a party will require the other party to agree to a liquidated damages clause in a contract. Most commonly, it occurs in a situation where a

Principal is purchasing goods or services from a Contractor.

This enables a Principal to place on record a genuine pre-estimate of the amount of damages or loss that it will suffer in the event of a breach by the Contractor. The estimate must be within certain limits and not "out of all proportion".

Liquidated damages can either be a stated dollar amount or an amount easily ascertainable by reference to a fixed scale of charges or by a simple calculation.

It is designed to overcome the necessity for a Principal to otherwise have to prove loss in a claim for damages. By doing so, it can save the Principal time and make the recovery proceedings considerably less expensive for a Principal.

The provision is becoming increasingly common in service contracts.

Penalty

If the agreed figure is not a genuine pre-estimate of the loss, it may be construed by a court to be a penalty. The generally accepted test of whether a liquidated damages claim amounts to a penalty is whether the amount claimed is "extravagant and unconscionable". The fact that it may be merely "unfair" may not be sufficient to move a court to strike such a clause down, as the parties will be required to stand by their bargain.

Depending upon the jurisdiction, penalties are generally *void* or *unenforceable* since they are said to be contrary to public policy. As this is a developing area of the law, you should check with your lawyer to establish the correct position for your particular jurisdiction.

Prudent practice (from a Contractor's perspective) requires that some form of *ceiling* or *cap* be placed on any total liquidated damages amount claimed by a Principal.

■ ■ ■

Force majeure clause

A simple *force majeure* clause often looks like this:

> *Neither party shall be liable for any failure or delay or default in performing hereunder if such failure or delay or default is caused by conditions beyond its control including, but not limited to Acts of God, Government restrictions, wars, insurrections and/or any other cause beyond the reasonable control of the party whose performance is affected.*

What it is used for and why

A *force majeure* event is an agreed event beyond the control of a party, which frustrates the ability of that party to perform its obligations under the contract.

The clause is intended to relieve that party from complying with its obligations under the contract for a certain period (usually, but not always, for the duration of the *force majeure* event).

In many jurisdictions, there is no law that defines what constitutes a *force majeure* event. It will usually depend upon what the parties can negotiate and agree upon.

Given the differences in the way *force majeure* is recognised in different jurisdictions, it is prudent practice to use the *force majeure* concept as a specifically defined term in a contract.

Depending on the circumstances of a particular transaction and how the parties view them, *force majeure* events can sometimes include strikes and industrial disputes, wars, riots, acts of God, etc.

In the context of a contract for the provision of services, a hotly debated *force majeure* point often is whether to include "strike or industrial dispute" in the definition.

On one side: the provider of services will argue that it will not be able to provide the services if a strike occurs, as it will not have the necessary personnel available.

On the other side: the recipient of the services often argues that it requires and is paying for an uninterrupted service. With this in mind, it is therefore, the contractor's role to manage such risks as part of its business.

Golden Rule

It is generally to the benefit of anyone supplying goods or providing a service to have a *force majeure* clause in their contract.

As a contractor or service provider, it is of benefit to make a *force majeure* clause as broad as possible. One way to do this is by adding a "catch-all" form of wording to the end of the definition section such as:

or any external event beyond the control of the parties

Of course, the converse applies if you are the recipient of a service. In which case, you will have an active interest in "tightening" the definition or even deleting the *force majeure* clause from the contract.

A properly drafted *force majeure* clause should consist of three sections:

1) **definition** of which events will constitute a *force majeure* event;

2) how and when the **notification** to the other party of such an event arising, should take place; and

3) **extent** of suspension of the obligations during a *force majeure* event.

A sample of a more elaborate *force majeure* clause, containing these three components, is shown below.

Definition

"Force Majeure Event" means any natural disaster, strike or other industrial action beyond the control of the Contractor, explosion, lightning, quarantine, epidemic, radiation, war, riot, terrorism, insurrection, Act of Parliament, act of God, valid direction by a Government Agency or any external event beyond the control of the Parties which frustrates the Contractor's ability to perform its obligations under this contract.

Notification

If a Force Majeure Event occurs and prevents the Contractor from performing in full any of its obligations under this Contract, the Contractor must notify the Principal of the nature of the Force Majeure Event, the time of its commencement and likely duration and the extent to which its obligations are effected.

Suspension of obligations

Provided that the Contractor notifies the Principal in accordance with this clause as soon as practicable after it becomes aware of a Force Majeure Event, its obligations under the Contract are suspended to the extent that the Contractor is prevented from performing them.

Mitigation

The Contractor must use its reasonable endeavours to overcome the effect of a Force Majeure Event notified to the Principal under this clause.

Right to make alternative arrangements

If a Force Majeure Event occurs which prevents the Contractor from performing all or any of the Services, the Principal may make alternative arrangements for the provision of those Services affected until the Force Majeure Event is overcome and the Principal may offset the reasonable costs of doing so against any fee payable by the Principal to the Contractor during that period.

Limits of the clause

In some jurisdictions (such as in the United Kingdom), a *force majeure* provision is likely to be subject to a reasonableness test. It is likely to be held to be reasonable if it is limited to events that are genuinely outside the control of the party relying on them.

■ ■ ■

Inadequacy of damages clause

The *inadequacy of damages* clause consists of an acknowledgment that a breach of contract may cause irreparable harm to the other party. The inadequacy of damages clause may look like this:

> *The Contractor acknowledges that damages are not a sufficient remedy for the Principal for any breach of this Agreement and the Principal is entitled to specific performance or an injunction or other equitable relief (as appropriate) as a remedy for any breach or threatened breach by the Contractor, in addition to any other remedies available at law or in equity to the Principal.*

What it is used for and why

Firstly, we shall define some key terminology to help you understand the material in this section. For simplicity, we have named the service provider the "Contractor" and the receiver of the services, the "Principal".

Some handy terms

Injunction

An *injunction* is a court order either:

- restraining or preventing someone from committing a particular act, whether existing or threatened. For example, a person might seek an injunction to prevent another from chopping down a tree or demolishing a building. These are sometimes called *prohibitory* injunctions as they prohibit someone from doing something.

- enjoining (or compelling) someone to do a particular act. For example, ordering a party to carry out a certain contractual obligation. These are sometimes called *mandatory* injunctions as they compel someone to actually do something.

Injunctions can be *interlocutory* or interim. These are generally urgent in nature and are granted pending a final hearing on whether the injunction should be permanent or final.

Injunctions can also be *permanent* or final. This is an order made by a court after a formal court hearing, where the court hears both parties' version of events and any legal argument.

The granting of an injunction is at the court's discretion.

> ### *Equitable relief*
>
> This refers to a court-ordered remedy not consisting of monetary damages. There are a number of different forms of equitable relief available.
>
> Generally, the most common forms of relief are injunctions (also called injunctive relief).
>
> Such relief is granted where an award of monetary damages would not be sufficient on its own to compensate an aggrieved party.

Now that we have covered some basic terminology, we can return to consider the *inadequacy of damages* clause.

Some agreements will contain an acknowledgment by one party that any breach of the agreement *may* cause irreparable harm to the other and that it will consent to the other party seeking injunctive relief.

Most jurisdictions will permit an aggrieved party to seek injunctive relief for the breach (or an anticipatory breach) of certain agreements. However, in order to successfully obtain such injunctive relief, the party seeking it will nevertheless need to demonstrate to the court that it will suffer irreparable harm if the conduct complained of is permitted, or permitted to continue.

It is acceptable to agree to a clause stating that:

In the event of any breach of this Agreement by the Contractor, the Principal **may** *suffer irreparable harm.*

However, you should generally not agree to wording to the effect that:

In the event of any breach of this Agreement by the Contractor, the Principal **will** *suffer irreparable harm.*

Remember, that in order to be successful in an application for an injunction, one of the things a Principal must prove is that an award of damages could not adequately compensate it for the harm it will suffer.

One view on accepting the wording that *the Principal* **will** *suffer irreparable harm* is that it could effectively save the Principal the trouble of having to prove to a court, that it would indeed suffer such irreparable harm.

Other lawyers would argue that the use of such words in an agreement would not be of benefit to a Principal. The legal rationale being that it is not possible to exclude (by the terms of a contract) a court's discretion and oblige a court to find that the balance of convenience would favour the granting of an injunction against a Contractor.

Assuming the latter position, that a court still required a Principal to actually prove irreparable damage, the wording could still certainly be used against the Contractor as *evidence of the intention* of the parties.

At the very least, it would be extremely awkward and embarrassing for a Contractor to then have to resile from such an acknowledgment in court.

However, the point should not be lost that to create such a situation of uncertainty is to almost invite litigation. Therefore, it is sensible practice to try and avoid such wording, wherever possible.

■■■

Joint and several liability clause

A *joint and several liability* clause may look something like this:

> In this Agreement, all covenants, agreements, undertakings, representations, warranties and indemnities by more than one person are given jointly and severally.

What it is used for and why

Firstly, it is necessary to understand what is meant by the term *joint and several liability*. This term often appears in contracts where there are two or more persons (or companies) as one party to a contract. For example, assume the parties to a contract are:

John Indett and **Mary Indett** *(the "Borrowers")*

borrowing money from:

Smackham Tillitt Hertz Finance Ltd *(the "Lender")*

Also, assume the contract provides that:

The **Borrowers** *shall be* <u>*jointly and severally liable*</u> *to the* **Lender***.*

In the event of default by *either or both* **John** and **Mary**, the **Lender** would be entitled to sue <u>either or both</u> **John** and **Mary**. The **Lender** would not need to sue them separately or individually.

The **Lender** could elect to sue *only* **John Indett** to recover its loss, if say, **Mary Indett** had disappeared or gone bankrupt.

It would then be entirely up to **John** to attempt to sue **Mary** to seek contribution from her, to apportion the loss evenly between them.

When used thoughtfully, such a simple clause can have very powerful effects.

A common area of usage of such a provision is in banking documentation. When there are two or more co-borrowers, the bank's loan documentation will always contain a joint and several liability provision, covering any default of any one borrower or all of the borrowers.

Similarly, where a property is being leased to two or more persons, a landlord will insist upon a joint and several liability clause. So that in the event of default, the landlord need only pursue the most accessible defendant. For example, if one of them were to "disappear".

The clause can also be useful in a sale of goods or for the provision of services. In fact, wherever there is a situation where one is dealing with two contractors on the other side in the one agreement, the clause can help avoid the possibility of having to "split" legal actions and having to pursue two separate parties in default.

Case study: in the frame

Joint and several liability clauses

Another situation in which the use of a joint and several liability clause is desirable is the case of a commercial television or radio station. To generate income, such stations rely upon advertisers running paid advertisements.

Often an advertiser might approach the station through an intermediary such as an advertising agency. In this example, the advertising agency provides a "turn-key" (complete) service to the advertiser and arranges for all aspects of production and placement of the advertisements.

The agency collects an all-inclusive fee from the advertiser and the advertiser expects the agency to remit any monies owing to the various parties involved (the television station, film production company, etc).

For the purposes of this example, assume there is a contract between:

- the television station;
- the agency; and
- the advertiser.

The contract, prepared by the television station's legal department, provides that the advertiser and the agency shall be jointly and severally liable to the television station.

In the event that the agency goes into bankruptcy or liquidation without having paid the television station, the television station has the added prospect of recovery from the advertiser, of any monies owing to the station.

This is despite the fact that the advertiser will have already paid the entire amount to the agency for disbursement to the various parties entitled.

Unfortunately, for the advertiser, it will face the prospect of having to pay twice for the same advertisement; once to the defunct agency and then again to the television station.

The television station has what amounts to a dual security for the payment of the outstanding sum.

If the advertiser had been the one to go into liquidation, before having paid the agency any monies, the television station would have been entitled to seek recovery of the amount owing to it under the contract, entirely from the agency.

When confronted with a request for the inclusion of a joint and several liability provision in a contract, you need to carefully consider:

1) How similar are the interests of the parties, who are joint and severally liable? For example, does one hold a 1% stake in the outcome and in return face a potential 100% risk?

2) What are the respective means of each party to become jointly and severally liable? This refers to the *actual* means, rather than the *apparent* ones. For example, there are many subsidiary companies of large household-name groups of companies that may be technically insolvent. The only way they maintain solvency is with parent company support. If that support stops, the subsidiary "dies" (along with your prospects of seeking any contribution for their share).

3) How stable are the other parties? Take heed of the favourite statement used in the securities and investment industry:

> *Past performance is no indicator or guarantee of future returns.*

Golden Rule

You must *never* agree to accept joint and several liability with another party (or parties), unless you are prepared to assume 100% of the liability.

Limitations of the clause

In the event that you are the one requiring two or more other parties to be jointly and severally liable to you, you should ensure that the clause contains express wording enabling you to release any of the others from liability without affecting the liability to you of the remainder.

> *The Lender may release settle or compromise, in whole or in part, the liability of any one or more Borrowers or may grant an extension of time or other indulgence to one or more Borrowers without affecting the liability of the other Borrowers.*

In the absence of such express wording, any settlement or compromise with one of the parties liable to you, could (depending upon the jurisdiction) potentially operate as a release to *all* other parties from liability to you.

■ ■ ■

Indemnity clause

An indemnity clause often looks like this:

> *The Contractor shall indemnify and hold harmless the Principal (including but not limited to the Principal's officers, employees, contractors and agents) against all losses, damages, costs or*

expenses which the Principal incurs or may incur
as a result of any act, omission, negligence or
breach of this Agreement by the Contractor.

When it is used and why

An indemnity is a contractual commitment by a
party to make good a specified loss suffered by the
other party. In other words, it is an acknowledgment and promise by one party to cover the
potential liability of another.

Careful attention must always be paid to
indemnity clauses as their impact can be far-
reaching and potentially devastating.

Notice the clause above does not contain
restrictions or limits upon:

- the types of losses sustained by the Principal;
- whether the obligation to indemnify is limited only to
  direct losses sustained by the Principal;
- whether the obligation to indemnify extends to
  include indirect (or consequential) losses or
  otherwise; or
- whether the obligation to indemnify arises only
  through the actions or inactions of the Contractor, or
  in combination with a third party.

A prudent Contractor would make the following
modifications to the above clause (note that deleted

words are shown as ~~strikethrough~~ text and added words are <u>underlined</u>):

> *The Contractor shall indemnify and hold harmless the Principal (including but not limited to the Principal's officers, employees, contractors and agents) against ~~all~~ losses, damages, costs or expenses which the Principal <u>directly and reasonably</u> incurs ~~or may incur~~ as a <u>direct</u> result of <u>and to the extent of</u> any act, omission, negligence or <u>material</u> breach of this Agreement by the Contractor <u>in connection with or arising out of the performance of the Services</u>. The Contractor's <u>obligation to indemnify shall not extend to include any indirect or consequential loss</u>.*

A key feature of an indemnity is that the obligation created by it can often extend *beyond* that which would otherwise be imposed on a party under the general law.

Typically, in a claim for a breach of contract against a Contractor, a Principal might not recover *all* of the loss incurred. The indemnity, however, will extend to cover losses that might not otherwise have been covered by a claim for damages for breach of the agreement. That is to say, in the event of a breach, the Contractor's damages' bill will generally be higher with an indemnity clause than without one.

For a Principal, the indemnity is a particularly attractive mechanism to outsource liability to a Contractor. This is because its very concept is to make the injured party whole again, as if the loss had not occurred, even if the person who agrees to indemnify would not otherwise have had any obligation to do so. This is particularly so in circumstances where it contains wording such as:

> *notwithstanding the negligence of the Principal or anyone acting under the Principal's authority*

OR

> *shall include any indirect or consequential loss suffered by the Principal or anyone claiming through the Principal*

A prudent Contractor must be aware of a Principal's attempts to outsource liability *beyond* the scope of the goods and/or services to be provided by the Contractor.

In a situation where a Contractor provides goods and/or services to a Principal, a typical indemnity clause will provide for the Contractor to indemnify the Principal against:

> *any damage, loss, cost, expense or liability incurred by the Principal arising from:*
>
> *(a) the provision of the goods and/or services;*
>
> *(b) any breach of the agreement; or*
>
> *(c) any act, omission or negligence*

caused by the Contractor, its employees, agents or sub-contractors.

When drafting or considering a draft of an indemnity clause, you should understand the main reasons they are generally deficient. There are usually five main reasons:

1) Liability extends well beyond the terms of the contract or even for negligence alone.

2) There is no exception for the negligent acts or omissions of third parties not under the direct control of the party giving the indemnity.

3) There is no exception for the negligence, acts or omissions of the other party to the contract.

4) There is no reduction in liability *to the extent* of negligence.

5) There is no specific and express exclusion for consequential or indirect loss or damage.

Golden Rule

In "plain English", in circumstances where it is appropriate, a balanced indemnity clause should apportion liability evenly as follows:

- if we mess up, we are responsible only for the direct consequences;

- if you mess up, you are responsible only for the direct consequences;

- if someone under our control is to blame, we are responsible for the direct consequences;

- if we share the blame, then we share responsibility, for the direct consequences, to the extent that we are each at fault; and

- if someone other than someone under our control is to blame, we are not responsible.

It is vitally important to have a lawyer carefully check any indemnity clause in a contract.

For a more comprehensive discussion on indemnity clauses and a demonstration of specific examples of the use of such clauses, you should consult **Understanding Indemnity Clauses**, the first volume in the *Commercial Contracts for Managers Series*.

■■■

Termination for convenience clause

A *termination for convenience* clause looks something like this:

> *The Principal may terminate the Contract at any time by giving* [for example, thirty (30) days] *written notice to the Contractor. The Contractor shall be entitled to payment for Services performed*

in the normal course until the date of termination, to the extent that the work has been performed satisfactorily.

What it is used for and why

A termination for convenience clause is not a "normal" commercial term. It tends to be found in almost every government contract, but increasingly corporations in the private sector are mimicking the trend for their use.

The rationale from a government perspective, is that long term contractual arrangements should not constrain a change in government or a change in government policy, that might otherwise cause a waste of taxpayers' money or burden a government with unneeded supplies or outmoded technology.

The termination for convenience clause grants an extremely broad right to terminate the other party's performance without being liable for breach-of-contract damages. The clause generally limits the ability of the party being terminated to recover only the costs incurred plus profits from work *completed*. The clause normally precludes the recovery of *anticipatory* profit.

In general, such clauses operate unilaterally (only one party can terminate the contract for convenience) and therefore do not give the other party the certainty of tenure that a "normal" contract does.

If that alone was not bleak enough for a party to a government contract, an additional clause supplementing the termination for convenience powers has found favour in government circles: essentially, the new clause provided that if a contract was ever incorrectly or improperly terminated for default or breach, then such termination would be deemed a termination for convenience. In effect, the clause automatically converts a wrongdoing on the part of government into a termination for convenience!

If you must absolutely accept a termination for convenience clause, you should seek to negotiate more favourable terms on, at least, the following matters:

- to include provision for reimbursement of the actual costs incurred in mobilising and demobilising in respect of any equipment and materials;

- to include provision for reimbursement of the costs of settling and paying termination settlements for staff dedicated to the contract;

- to include provision for reimbursement of the costs of settling and paying termination settlements for sub-contractors dedicated to the contract; and

- to attempt to lengthen the term of notice from the ubiquitous 30 days to, say, 90 or even 180 days.

■ ■ ■

Alternative dispute resolution (ADR) clause

There are a number of variations on the alternative dispute resolution theme. They range from a simple escalation of the matter to the CEOs of the parties for good faith negotiations, to more elaborate mediation or arbitration procedures:

DISPUTES

All disputes, differences and questions arising out of, in connection or in relation to this Agreement shall be settled by mutual discussions between the parties in good faith. However if no such settlement is reached within one month, the matter shall be referred to the Chief Executive of each party who shall attempt to resolve the matter in good faith within one further month.

The most common form (and often the least expensive) of ADR methods is a reference of the matter in dispute to a mediator. The clause sets out the steps the parties must follow:

DISPUTES

a. *If there is a dispute between the parties concerning this Agreement, then the parties must attempt to resolve any such dispute by the mediation procedure set out herein.*

b.   *The mediation procedure is as follows:*

   i.   *a meeting must be held between the Chief Operating Officer of the respective parties, with a view to resolving the dispute prior to any further action being taken;*

   ii.   *if the dispute is not resolved within a period of 14 days of the meeting between the parties' respective Chief Executive Officers, either party may start mediation by serving a mediation notice on the other party;*

   iii.   *the mediation notice must state that a dispute has arisen and identify what the dispute is;*

   iv.   *the parties must jointly request the appointment of a mediator and failing agreement within seven (7) days of service of the mediation notice, either party may apply to the President of the Law Society of New South Wales to appoint a mediator;*

   v.   *once the mediator has accepted the appointment, the parties must comply with the mediator's instructions; and*

   vi.   *if a dispute is not resolved within 30 days of the appointment of the mediator, or any other period agreed by the parties in writing, mediation ceases.*

c.   *The mediator may fix the charges for the mediation which must be paid equally by the parties.*

d.   *If the dispute is settled, all parties must sign the terms of agreement and those terms are binding on the parties.*

e. *The mediation is confidential and statements made by the mediator or the parties, as well as discussions between the participants to the mediation before, after or during the mediation cannot be used in legal proceedings.*

f. *It shall be a term of the engagement of the mediator that the parties release the mediator from any court proceedings relating to the dispute or the mediation.*

g. *The mediator is not bound by the rules of natural justice and may discuss the dispute with a party in the absence of any other party.*

What it is used for and why

Methods other than traditional litigation in courts are becoming increasingly popular, particularly as they can often provide solutions more quickly and at lower costs.

ADR methods tend to have the benefits of confidentiality and informality. Everything that is said or disclosed is not a matter of public record as it would be in most traditional courts.

Also the savings in legal costs can be considerable. However, such cost savings can be negated in the instance where an arbitration hearing is repeated by reference of the matter to a court for what will effectively be a rehearing.

The most often used lines of ADR in escalating order are:

1) **Good faith negotiations:** between the chief executive officers of each party and perhaps (in some circumstances) a lawyer/s.

2) **Mediation:** which is becoming a more popular method. This involves the use of an independent and impartial mediator whose role is to encourage the parties to find positive ways of resolving their differences in an amicable and non-confrontational way. The mediator does not provide a binding decision at the end of the mediation but if the final settlement terms arrived at are acceptable, the parties can agree to be bound by them.

3) **Arbitration:** is almost akin to a private and slightly less formal trial. Procedure and rules of evidence are generally adhered to in arbitration proceedings. An arbitrator is appointed who (similarly to a judge in a court) hears the evidence, rules on objections during the hearing and will make findings of fact and issue a decision on the dispute. Depending upon the jurisdiction, there may be:

   • a right to have the matter reheard in court;

   • a limited right of appeal to a court; or

- a prohibition on any appeal or rehearing of the matter in a court.

Parties can agree to use any one of these methods to deal with a dispute, or a combination of methods. For example, before resorting to litigation, a contract might provide that the parties have negotiations between CEOs. If that proves unsuccessful, they must then proceed to the next step and have the matter mediated.

There may be a provision in a contract preventing recourse to a court before exhausting all of the prescribed ADR remedies. An exception to such a clause for "urgent interlocutory applications" is generally a wise inclusion.

One of the difficulties with ADR is that the methods may not always be as final and conclusive as they are in traditional courts. The issue of arbitrated determinations being final and binding upon the parties can sometimes tend to be problematic, depending upon the jurisdiction.

It is important to also be aware that arbitration awards may not be enforceable in certain other jurisdictions. This consideration is particularly relevant where the other party is a foreign entity.

You should ensure that you seek advice from a qualified lawyer in the appropriate jurisdiction/s applicable to your contract, before consenting to the inclusion of ADR clauses into a contract, particularly where such clauses attempt to usurp or oust the jurisdiction of the courts.

Golden Rule

It is always important to place strict *time limits* on ADR procedures, especially where court proceedings must be deferred until after the prescribed ADR avenues have been exhausted.

The absence of time limits, for example could theoretically prolong "good faith negotiations between the parties" indefinitely.

Chapter 8

CONCLUSION

■ ■ ■

Commercial contracts do not need to be unnecessarily complex in order to be effective.

However, there are certain safeguards and protections that are necessary and desirable. As you can see, many of them can be easily included into an agreement.

You have seen demonstrations of some of the fundamentals, to enable you to detect when these safeguards might be missing or might only apply unilaterally. You have also seen when their use may have been overzealous and ambitious.

We commenced with the basics and dissected a commercial contract into its individual component parts. This enabled you to understand where boilerplate clauses fit in to the general scheme of contracts.

You have by now gained an understanding of the importance of correctly naming parties to a contract in boilerplate clauses and ensuring they have adequate substance and means, in order to be able to meet any of their obligations. To cater for those situations where the means and substance of a company are in doubt, we have briefly examined the areas in which one may seek adequate assurance by way of a bank or parent company guarantee.

You have gained an appreciation of the significance of making any term of a contract into an essential term. This should be useful information to have when it is being done to you. Equally, you may have a need to require the timing of another's performance of a task to be made into an essential term of the contract.

Some of the boilerplate clauses used to protect intellectual property have also been covered. As you have seen, the exact nature of the protection required will depend upon the circumstances. However, there are a number of ways to safeguard your ownership of valuable intellectual property.

The reach of boilerplate clauses extends from basic (but, by no means, trivial) administrative tasks such as the correct manner of service of notices, to harnessing the vast power of indemnity clauses (to which an entire volume in this series has been dedicated). Just in case you thought giving a notice was a trivial task, try getting it wrong and see the consequences. For example, ask the employer who was required to pay 30 months severance to a high-priced executive, instead of the contractually-mandated six months; all because they gave the employee his termination notice two weeks late — *after* his contract had automatically rolled over for a further two years! Ouch.

Looking at another (on the surface) seemingly trivial issue: *jurisdiction*. I have personally witnessed organisations spending, quite literally and without exaggeration, millions of dollars on this point alone. Jurisdiction is the type of area that becomes horrendously expensive to manage in practice. It usually involves having to fly professors of law or very senior counsel first-class to another country to explain the law of one country to a judge in another country, who must then apply that foreign law to the facts of the case (remembering also that the facts of the case will often also be in dispute). Combining all of these complications with one other: the other side's expert (equally, if not even more, eminent and expensive than yours), will almost certainly be contradicting your expert's position.

All of this becomes a colossal drain on company resources and a great experience for the lawyers involved. Remember, when the person with experience meets the person with the money, the result usually is that the person with the experience gets the money and the person with the money gets the experience.

As you can see, there are a great number of matters dealt with in any negotiation culminating in a contract. A number of fundamental issues do not commonly arise *during* the negotiation. Such issues tend to appear in the first draft of the contract document. As such, there may be a tendency to relegate these issues to "second-rate" status, in the minds of the parties. A time-conscious executive might be tempted to think:

> *If these issues were important, we would have covered them during the negotiation.*

It can be a dangerous practice to allow yourself to be lured into such a trap. The reason such issues are not commonly raised or discussed during a negotiation is that their effect hinges very much on the way they are drafted into a contract.

This is one of the reasons why it is wise to seek to have control of the contract drafting process, wherever possible.

It is important for you as managers representing your company in a negotiation, not to disengage yourselves, at this point.

These are issues requiring (and deserving of) your attention and familiarity.

More often than not, you will be working with your lawyer on the finer drafting nuances of the various clauses. Whilst the drafting of such clauses is often left to the lawyers to negotiate and finalise, you should monitor and continue to be a part of this process.

Boilerplate clauses might seem standard and "run of the mill", but their correct use can often be *pivotal* in holding a contract together and ensuring that the deal terms unfold as originally planned.

INDEX

OTHER TITLES IN THE SERIES

Before you sign a contract understand its essential elements. There are also tip and hints about the many pitfalls and advice on avoiding future disputes.

ISBN: 978-085297-773-6   224 pages

You've been involved in weeks, or sometimes even months, of hardfought negotiations. However, the deal is not done until until the final form of contract is agreed upon and executed. You have to have a basic understanding of commercial contracts every step of the way.

ISBN: 978-0-85297-720-0   278 pages

This book explains the essential elements necessary for a complete confidentiality agreement. You will learn how unscrupulous players use confidentiality agreements to gain an unfair advantage, and how to avoid getting "caught".

ISBN: 978-0-85297-757-6   116 pages

This book explains the differences between fair indemnity clauses and those that are unduly onerous and will give readers an understanding of the nature of indemnities and their potentially devastating effects.

ISBN: 978-0-85297-760-6   104 pages

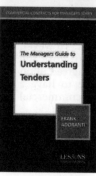

Samples of tender conditions and documents are included to illustrate to the manager capital expenditure, protection of intellectual property and variations to the scopes of works and pricing. The book also explains legal issues, such as liquidated damages, force majeure, indemnities, and so on.

ISBN: 978-0-85297-761-3   164 pages